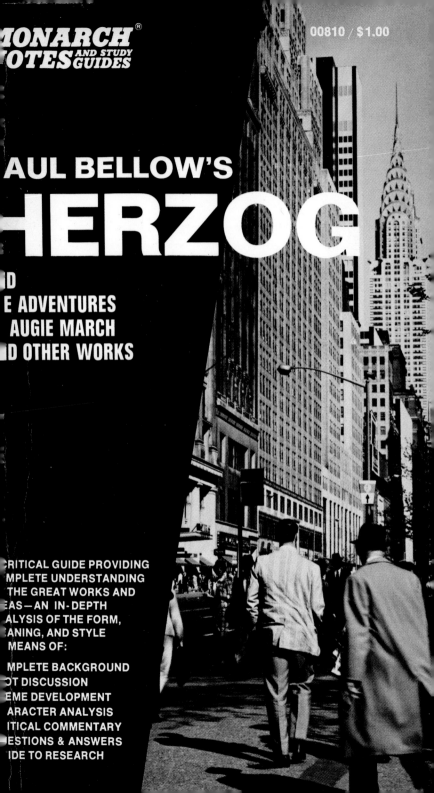

MONARCH HIGH SCHOOL STUDY GUIDES

IBM #	$1.25 Each Unless Otherwise Indicated
	LANGUAGE
00115	SPANISH—ONE YEAR
00107	SPANISH—TWO YEARS
00114	SPANISH—THREE YEARS
00113	FRENCH—ONE YEAR
00108	FRENCH—TWO YEARS ($1.50)
00109	FRENCH—THREE YEARS ($1.50)
00116	LATIN—ONE YEAR
00117	LATIN—TWO YEARS
00132	LATIN—THREE YEARS
00128	GERMAN—ONE YEAR
00129	GERMAN—TWO YEARS
	MATHEMATICS
00123	7th-8th GRADE MATH
00118	ELEMENTARY ALGEBRA
00119	INTERMEDIATE ALGEBRA

IBM #	$1.25 Each Unless Otherwise Indicated
00110	GEOMETRY ($1.50)
00121	11th YEAR MATH ($1.50)
00120	TRIGONOMETRY
00126	ADVANCED ALGEBRA ($1.50)
	ENGLISH
00125	ENGLISH—TWO YEARS
00106	ENGLISH—THREE YEARS
00111	ENGLISH—FOUR YEARS ($1.50)
	HISTORY
00101	AMERICAN HISTORY
00102	WORLD HISTORY ($1.50)
00122	GEOGRAPHY ($1.50)
00131	AMERICAN HISTORY AND WORLD BACKGROUNDS ($1.50)

IBM #	$1.25 Each Unless Otherwise Indicated
00133	AMERICAN GOVERNMENT ($1.50)
00134	CITIZENSHIP EDUCATION ($1.50)
	SCIENCE
00103	ELEMENTARY BIOLOGY
00104	CHEMISTRY ($1.50)
00105	PHYSICS
00112	EARTH SCIENCE ($1.50)
00124	GENERAL SCIENCE
	ECONOMICS & BUSINESS
00127	BUSINESS ARITHMETIC
00135	BOOKKEEPING

MONARCH LITERATURE NOTES

IBM #	$1.00 Each Unless Otherwise Indicated
00800	ADAMS—The Education of Henry Adams
00801	AESCHYLUS—The Plays
00802	AMERICAN POLITICAL DOCUMENTS ($1.50)
00524	AMERICAN POLITICAL PHILOSOPHY
00803	ANDERSON—Winesburg, Ohio
00805	ARISTOPHANES—The Plays
00506	ARISTOTLE—The Philosophy ($1.50)
00793	ARNOLD—The Poetry
00791	AUDEN—The Poetry
00704	AUSTEN—Emma, Mansfield Park
00801	AUSTEN—Pride and Prejudice
00806	BACON—The Writings
00807	BALDWIN—The Major Works (Go Tell It on the Mountain and other works)
00808	BALZAC—Eugénie Grandet, Père Goriot
00809	BEAT LITERATURE
00756	BECKETT—Waiting for Godot and other works
00810	BELLOW—The Major Novels (Herzog, Adventures of Augie March, and other works)
00550	BEOWULF
00525	BERKELEY—The Philosophy
00775	BLAKE—The Poetry
00811	BOSWELL—Life of Johnson
00551	BRECHT—The Plays
00602	BRONTE, C.—Jane Eyre
00603	BRONTE, E.—Wuthering Heights
00776	BROWNING, ROBERT—The Poetry
00657	BUCK—The Good Earth
00819	BURDICK and LEDERER—The Ugly American
00757	CAMUS—The Stranger
00552	CAMUS—The Major Works
00604	CATHER—My Antonia and other works
00553	CERVANTES—Don Quixote
00511	CHAUCER—Canterbury Tales
00554	CHEKHOV—The Plays
00815	CLARK—The Ox-Bow Incident
00526	CLASSICAL ECONOMISTS
00778	COLERIDGE—The Rime of the Ancient Mariner and other poems
00522	COMMUNIST THEORY FROM MARX TO MAO ($1.50)
00816	CONNELL—Green Pastures
00817	CONRAD—Heart of Darkness, The Secret Sharer

IBM #	$1.00 Each Unless Otherwise Indicated
00605	CONRAD—Lord Jim and other works
00606	CONRAD—Victory, Nostromo, Nigger of the Narcissus, and The Shadow-Line
00884	CONSTITUTION—Leading Cases ($1.50)
00658	COOPER—The Deerslayer
00659	COOPER—The Last of the Mohicans
00818	COOPER—The Pathfinder
00813	COOPER—The Pioneers
00779	CRANE, HART—The Poetry
00660	CRANE—Red Badge of Courage
00819	CUMMINGS—The Poetry
00820	DANA—Two Years Before the Mast
00510	DANTE—The Divine Comedy
00555	DARWIN AND SPENCER
00705	DEFOE—Moll Flanders
00821	DEFOE—Robinson Crusoe
00527	DESCARTES—The Philosophy
00607	DEWEY—The Writings
00608	DICKENS—Bleak House
00822	DICKENS—A Christmas Carol, The Chimes
00609	DICKENS—David Copperfield
00610	DICKENS—Great Expectations
00823	DICKENS—Hard Times
00824	DICKENS—Oliver Twist
00706	DICKENS—Pickwick Papers
00611	DICKENS—A Tale of Two Cities
00780	DICKINSON—The Poetry
00731	DONNE—The Poetry and the metaphysical poets
00825	DOS PASSOS—U.S.A. and other works
00556	DOSTOYEVSKY—Brothers Karamazov
00517	DOSTOYEVSKY—Crime and Punishment
00558	DOSTOYEVSKY—Notes from the Undeground
00557	DOSTOYEVSKY—The Idiot
00661	DREISER—An American Tragedy
00662	DREISER—Sister Carrie
00781	DRYDEN—The Poetry
00826	EARLY CHURCH FATHERS—The Writings ($1.50)
00707	EIGHTEENTH-CENTURY RESTORATION PLAYS ($1.95)
00708	ELIOT—Adam Bede
00709	ELIOT—Middlemarch
00710	ELIOT—Mill on the Floss
00612	ELIOT—Silas Marner

IBM #	$1.00 Each Unless Otherwise Indicated
00782	ELIOT, T. S.—Murder in the Cathedral and selected poems
00663	EMERSON—The Writings
00829	EURIPIDES—The Plays
00508	EURIPIDES, AESCHYLUS, AND ARISTOPHANES—The Plays
00830	EUROPEAN LITERATURE—Medieval to Neoclassic ($1.95)
00664	FAULKNER—Absalom, Absalom!
00665	FAULKNER—As I Lay Dying
00666	FAULKNER—Light in August
00559	FEDERALIST PAPERS
00711	FIELDING—Joseph Andrews
00614	FIELDING—Tom Jones
00667	FITZGERALD—The Great Gatsby
00668	FITZGERALD—Tender Is the Night
00560	FLAUBERT—Madame Bovary, The Three Tales
00831	FORBES—Johnny Tremain
00712	FORSTER—Passage to India, Howards End
00561	FRANK—Diary of a Young Girl
00832	FRANKLIN—Autobiography
00833	FRENCH LITERATURE ($1.95)
00615	FREUD—The Writings
00767	FROMM—The Writings
00783	FROST—The Poetry
00835	GIDE—The Immoralist, Strait Is the Gate
00521	GOETHE—Faust
00836	GOETHE—Sorrows of Young Werther
00893	GOLDING—The Inheritors, Free Fall
00616	GOLDING—Lord of the Flies and other works
00892	GOLDING—Pincher Martin
00837	GOLDSMITH—She Stoops to Conquer and other works
00755	GOLDSMITH—The Vicar of Wakefield
00500	GREEK AND ROMAN CLASSICS ($2.95)
00838	GREENE—The Major Works (The Power and the Glory and other works)
00669	HALE—Man Without a Country
00890	HARDY—Far from the Madding Crowd
00713	HARDY—Jude the Obscure
00617	HARDY—The Mayor of Casterbridge
00618	HARDY—The Return of the Native

Continued on inside back cover

1704331

CONTENTS

INTRODUCTION

BIOGRAPHY

EARLY LIFE: A Canadian by birth, Saul Bellow was born in Lachine, Quebec, on July 10, 1915, the son of Abraham and Liza (Gordon) Bellow. He was one of several Bellow children who shared the poverty and uncertainty of Jewish immigrant life in the first quarter of this century. His mother was a hard worker who toiled at home for her husband and children, never quite understanding the strain and duress which beset the European-born in the New World. The father, ambitious but easily victimized by circumstance coupled with his own somewhat flamboyant nature, lived more on expectation and financial risk than on regularly remunerative endeavors. Thus the family's relative hand-to-mouth existence brought with it extremes of hardship and stress. However, there existed a warmth among the children and a sympathetic sharing of burdens and pleasures which characterizes immigrant life of that era.

LIFE IN CHICAGO: At an early age, Saul moved to Chicago with his family. The move from Canada was prompted by severe financial reverses and the dream of America popular among European immigrants. At least in America, it was thought, one had unlimited opportunity. As residents of the poorer section of Chicago, life was not noticeably easier for the Bellows. Although the children were growing up and could begin to contribute to the family income by securing part-time jobs, this did not ease the family's finances sufficiently. The economy of the country soon lost its wartime (World War I) prosperity and the Great Depression was imminent. At the same time, the children were restricted in the jobs available because of their obligations at school. Relations and friends extended their generosity from time to time, but finances still remained uncertain. Life in Chicago at this time was interesting and rich with opportunities for experience and observation to the sensitive and imaginative youth Saul seemed to be. At this time in Chicago's history, another element was added to life in the already colorful city—the nation's railroad and meat-packing center. For this was the era of large-scale crime, and Chicago abounded in criminal gangs of international fame. The mercurial careers of gangland notables were fodder for the public imagination. The city buzzed with an undercurrent of gossip concerning syndicated crime. One could observe an opulent and secure thug one day only to read about (and occasionally witness) his machine-gun demise the next. Such an atmosphere was bound to make life exciting, if not terrifying.

However, the Bellows adhered to their values of hard labor and its honest rewards. Despite the prolonged absence of the father from the family, necessitated by his attempts to provide them with that long dreamed of fortune, life afforded a sufficient if occasionally wanting existence. The children attained hard-won maturity and independence, while remaining financially responsible for the mother and those still at home. The sympathy and warmth of feeling for each other's needs and experiences was an important factor in Saul's development and can be seen in various aspects of his subsequent writings.

EDUCATION: It is fortunate that financial strain and domestic responsibility did not prevent the intelligent, sensitive young Bellow from pursuing his intellectual curiosity. He was able to finish high school, and in 1933, at the age of eighteen, he entered the University of Chicago. He remained there until 1935 and received his Bachelor of Science degree in 1937 from Northwestern University.

MARRIAGE AND EARLY CAREER: He was married on New Year's Eve of that same year to Anita Goshkin. In 1938, he became a teacher at Pestalozzi-Froebel Teachers College in Chicago—a position he retained until 1942. His first published work appeared in 1940. From 1943 to 1946 Bellow served as a member of the editorial department of the Encyclopedia Britannica. In 1944 his first novel, *Dangling Man*, was published. From 1944 to 1945, he fulfilled his wartime obligation with the

Maritime Service. In 1946 the author was appointed to the faculty of the University of Minnesota at Minneapolis as a teacher in the English Department. The following year his second novel, *The Victim*, was published. In 1948, Bellow was made an Assistant Professor of English and Guggenheim Fellow at Bradford College, Yale University. Under the Fellowship, he was able to spend a year in Paris where he began to write his best known early work, *The Adventures of Augie March*, which was published in 1953 and won the National Book Award for Fiction in 1954. From 1950 until 1952, when he received a National Institute of Arts and Letters Award, Bellow was a visiting lecturer at New York University. The following year he was appointed to the position of Creative Writing Fellow at Princeton University. From 1953 until 1954, he served on the faculty of Bard College in Annandale-on-Hudson, New York. He then returned as Assistant Professor of English to the University of Minnesota and was again a Guggenheim Fellow from 1955 to 1956. His fourth novel, *Seize the Day*, was published in 1956.

LATER EVENTS AND WORKS: Despite his professional growth and success, all matters did not go so well for the author. During this period of literary productivity, his marriage was terminated, leaving his son Gregory in the custody of the mother. In 1956, Bellow remarried. Another son, Adam, was the product of this union with Alexandra Tschachasov. The marriage, however, did not last. Bellow continued to enjoy professional success. In 1959, his fifth novel, *Henderson the Rain King*, was published. From 1959 to 1961, the author was the recipient of a Ford Foundation grant. In 1960 he was presented with the Friends of Literature Award for Fiction. Professional success was met with personal achievement in his third marriage in 1961 to Susan Glassman. The production of his play *The Upper Depths* during the 1963-64 Broadway season met with minimal success. In his accomplished metier of fiction, Bellow's crowning achievement to date was the publication of his sixth and most recent novel, *Herzog*.

CURRENT STATUS: Saul Bellow has been a prolific writer of both fiction and criticism since his first published piece appeared in 1940. His work has appeared widely in such publications as *Partisan Review, Hudson Review, Sewanee Review, New Yorker, New Republic, New Leader, Saturday Review, The Nation,* and *Esquire.* His literary undertakings have also included the co-editorship of *The Noble Savage,* a small literary magazine devoted to the works of contemporary authors. In addition to the numerous awards he has received, Saul Bellow maintains memberships in the Authors League, Yaddo Corporation, and the National Institute of Arts and Letters. One of the most prolific and influential authors in America, he currently makes his home in Tivoli, New York.

AMERICAN LITERATURE SINCE WORLD WAR II

EFFECTS OF WAR: During World War II, publishing was understandably interrupted and redirected by the violent changes in the artists' view of the world. For the most part, journalism and propaganda were superimposed over literature during the years of global conflict (1939-1945). Nonfiction supplanted fiction in the public's reading tastes, and moving pictures were a primary source of entertainment, for they offered the visual and physical escape required by the strain of war. Military and political matters demanded collective action on an international scale and the sensibilities of the artist reflected this suspension of primary individuality in favor of the interdependence of mankind made evident by the war. A unity of emotion and objective grew out of war's emphasis on survival. It was in this sense of collectiveness and cohesiveness that propagandistic literature and journalistic efforts to communicate replaced the traditional American pattern of rugged individualism in literature.

WAR'S END: Immediately after the cessation of hostilities there was a resurgence of individual concerns. Each writer had his own reflections on the war to communicate, from either direct or related experience. However unique was each writer's reaction to the war, there was a unifying effect of the holocaust on the sensibilities of men the world over. The result was a sense of alienation reflected in the prose and poetry of writers attempting to re-relate themselves to a world whose values the war had severely altered. The war proved the dominance of machine over man and of man's own potential for inhumanity.

As the last shreds of nineteenth-century idealism disintegrated, they were replaced by a skepticism for man's chances of survival coupled with a sense of his exile from a hostile world. Thus a new individualism was born—one of insecurity, doubt, and alienation. With the termination of war, each nation retreated from emergency international alliances into its own political and economic problems. But old institutions had been destroyed and new norms had to be developed. Hence, a progression from a literature reflecting world chaos to one portraying post-war decay.

DECADENCE AND RADICALISM: Such dissatisfaction and disillusionment as prevailed immediately after the war brought with it various attempts by writers to reach for a panacea. As such, these attempts were gropings backward for cure-alls of the past: religion, pre-war toughness, mysticism, and the false idealism attendant on immediate involvement with war. But when it was over, nothing was better. The sensibilities had not caught up with themselves. So they turned inward rather than outward, for the present was disillusioning and the future opaque. The post-war literary hero became either an overstimulated civilian still frantically motivated by the war, or a neurotic individual whose position as a bystander to it all was symptomatic of a morally undetermined world which precluded men of action and thus reinforced post-war neuroses. When all around were signs of decay, the protagonist could but stand there wincing, condemning, and asking himself, as well as the world, for a way out of the dilemma. The alternative was radical action born of dissatisfaction and despair, and yet disdainful of wartime collectiveness. Such was the condition of literature among the older generation of writers. (Hemingway, Dos Passos, Wolfe, Faulkner, and Fitzgerald).

THE NEW GENERATION: Immediately after the war there emerged a new group of important writers who added a new dimension to the realistic-naturalistic tradition in American fiction. The effects of war and its aftermath can be found in these writers' tone of detachment, their sense of disenchantment, and the dearth of sentimentality and overt emotional concern. The first crop of novelists, Jones, Shaw and Mailer, wrote about the adjustments to war and its aftermath. The protagonist of these novels is no less confused about his relationship to the world than he was before the war. However, the newer novelists employed a "patterned" technique, in which the differing backgrounds and reactions of characters are presented in comparison and contrast to that of the protagonist. This newer technique can be traced to the cinema whose influence was just beginning to make itself felt as a model for literature (rather than the reverse as had formerly been the case). Moreover, this new technique afforded a greater opportunity to present a quantitative impression of depersonalization and dislocation—two major aspects of war which concerned this group of writers.

CONTINUITY AND INNOVATION: The resemblance of the new generation of post-war writers to earlier American naturalism and realism could be seen in their attitudes of skepticism, materialism, and hard-minded anti-Puritanism as well as in the cynical, anti-heroic treatment of the military hierarchy and middle-class banality. As with their predecessors, the new post-war writers wrote an idiom of the "typically American" hard-boiled, terse, understated vernacular. The major difference between the post-World War I and the post-World War II writer is one of perspective. The earlier group lived in the shadow of global war and was further disillusioned by the Great Depression which followed. The impact of their work in tone and innovation was far greater. The great technical innovators of the so-called "lost-generation" were Hemingway, Faulkner, Cummings, and Dos Passos as well as others. For them, idiosyncrasy and defiance was the direct result of situations previously unexperienced by Americans. For the post-World War II writers, war was not a novel experience and thus did not require a revolution in technical presentation. Moreover, these writers were schooled in the techniques of their predecessors which had, for them, become somewhat conventional. Hence, the areas for innovation open to the new post-war authors were those of content and perspective. The individual, neo-romantic hero became the multiple hero or the non-hero in mass society, or the frustrated, alienated hero depressed and demoralized in an absurd world. New social questions regarding minority groups such as Jews and Negroes became important issues stemming from Hitler's anti-Semitism and segregation in the

Armed Forces. The limited scope and perspective of the earlier novels, reflecting past American isolationism and a hope for its return, gave way in post-World War II fiction to internationalism, social mass, and cultural heterodoxy. Although the new writers were deprived of the dramatic value of being the first post-war writers, they had the advantage of the earlier men's experiences to weave into their own and a point from which to depart. There were four major achievements of the immediate post-war group of writers: 1) an assertion of the need for belief in a context in which belief is almost impossible; 2) the adaptation of journalism and the techniques of their innovative predecessors to their experiences and reactions to war; 3) the emergence of a new type of protagonist with a new attitude; 4) an altered and enlarged scope for exploiting standard material as well as nascent subject matter—homosexuality, racial conflict, and advanced psychological abnormality.

PROTEST AND EXPLORATION: What emerged in literature from the immediate post-war period was a heterodox approach to the confusion and conflict of values, ideals, and systems. Most writers have been mainly concerned with the individual in terms of the mass. The diversity of approach can be seen in the multitudinous "isms" and "ologies" which reflect the state of chaos to which the contemporary world admits. From a revival of scrupulous orthodoxy to the most radical nihilism, writers since the Fifties have voiced their heterogeneous protest against modern distractions and seemingly ubiquitous chaos. The interesting thing is that while each writer has analyzed, illustrated, or explained a point of view, the literature of the last decade and a half has refrained from the confidence and didacticism of the past; instead it has anxiously expressed itself on a take-it-or-leave-it basis. This possibility for multiple interpretation has been contemporary literature's chief appeal for a highly literate and wide-reading public who themselves do not subscribe to a singular value system. People mainly want to understand, and the variety of explanations available in contemporary literature, while not providing THE answer, at least keeps alive the hope for an answer.

EXISTENTIALISM: A prevailing trend in post-war literature has been the expression of the philosophy of existentialism, which began with the Danish philosopher, Soren Kierkegaard in the nineteenth century. His position was that man exists by chance alone and needs to exist within himself, as the sole judge of his actions, rather than as an integral part of society with reciprocal rights and obligations. The essential subjectivity of man as a law unto himself frees him from the role of participator in a chaotic world symptomatic of the larger absurdity of existence itself. Man's existence is basically a suspension in a state of anxiety between the impersonal (and absurd) factors of birth and death. Therefore, man's real function is non-participation. The existentialist point of view was understandably adaptable to the post-war state of mind. It suited both the pre-war writer of decadence and the post-war radical, both of whom rejected the world as it was and sought a retreat from the paradoxes of humanist idealism and unavoidable skepticism. As redefined by Jean-Paul Sartre and other post-war French writers, existentialism has come to maintain that man's moral and social problems are mutually exclusive. American writers have adapted related aspects of Kierkegaard's philosophy to their work rather than the hard-core existentialism of their European contemporaries.

THE BEAT GENERATION: One of the most violent rejections of society can be found in the Beat movement of the Fifties. Among other things, this was a reaction against all social, political, and cultural tradition, taking on the hue of nihilism as it snowballed and eventually split into other forms of protest. Characterized by violence and absurdity, the Beats wanted to show the state of non-existence to which the individual had been reduced, victimized by mammoth institutions and systems of non-existent value. The howl of the Beats was led by the poet, Alan Ginsberg, and created in the novel by Jack Kerouac and others. The very nature of the Beats' rage was indicative of a deeply wounded sense of individuality refusing to be annihilated in spite of the odds. The "no value" cult was indicative of an incubation period in which new, operative values germinated to replace the old, defunct ones. The Beat movement, in a sense, may be considered America's answer to post-war European existentialism.

PSYCHOLOGY: While psychological literature has been in existence since the tragedies of ancient Greece, its dominance has been evident since the publication of Flaubert's *Madame Bovary*. That nineteenth-century work heralded the advent of realism, which has been the preponderant trend in literature since. As a mainstream, realism has had attendant currents of naturalism, regionalism, and psychological analysis. We think of *Madame Bovary* as a prototype of the combination of realism, naturalism, and psychology—a work which changed the course of the modern novel. Psychological literature can be defined in many senses with varying shades of meaning. Primarily, such literature emphasizes the inner conflicts of the characters by revealing to the reader the motivation and analysis of the action taken. Usually the character must work his way out of a dilemma in which universal values conflict with the dictates of the immediate situation; the dilemma is further complicated by the pressures of other characters in similar states of conflict. Moral and ethical decisions are then seen in terms of human psychology rather than as abstractions dictated solely by an impersonal force such as tradition, custom, or superstition.

DIVERSITY: The general acceptance of Freudian and other schools of psychology has further implemented the development of psychological literature. Man's consciousness of his environment and his various reactions to it have been widely presented from the internal or psychological point of view by numerous authors employing various techniques. These range from the conventionally discursive (such as Edith Wharton; to the highly experimental "stream of consciousness" (innovated by James Joyce). As psychology has played an even greater role in man's explanation of himself in relation to his environment, the psychological approach has gained greater prevalence in literature. The acceptance of psychology as a recognized science has resulted in the acceptance of the psychological approach in realistic and naturalistic literature. Thus, writers are able to approach the analysis of man's inner conflicts with diversity of technique and context, since art and science may be related in an infinite number of ways.

ABNORMALITY: Whether art shapes or reflects the consciousness of man is a rhetorical question; however the results of the relationship are more easily determinable. As science has developed, man's awareness of himself and his world has effected the removal of taboos from art. In literature this may be seen in the numerous subjects now written about that were previously repressed. As values change, so does behavior. The effect on literature has been particularly noticeable in the open presentation of such subjects as psychological abnormality and sex. Pioneers in the treatment of mental aberraticn date from the nineteenth century and include Poe, Dostoievsky, and Baudelaire among others. The moral dilemma and anxiety of the twentieth century have been treated psychologically by James Joyce and D. H. Lawrence and in the most contemporary offerings by William Faulkner and Carson McCullers. The growing emphasis has been away from a resolution in favor of restraint to the actual admission and avowal of neurosis and abnormality as contingent conditions of modern man. Such topics as homosexuality, sadism, masochism, paranoia and hypersexuality can be found in abundance between the covers of almost any contemporary work of literature. Whether secondary or primary to the author's major theme, psychology has played a crucial role in the development of twentieth-century literature. Since World War II, even more freedom has been granted to certain subjects in literature. The psychological school has enabled authors to draw attention to the inner aspects of human motivation in such a manner that the reader becomes mentally involved as a participator in the work instead of remaining outside as an observer. The diversity in approach and emphasis is great; however, such authors as Henry Miller, Truman Capote, Vladimir Nabokov, and Gore Vidal, among numerous others, represent that group of current writers in America who have successfully exposed formerly restricted areas in their effective literary presentations of psychological abnormality.

PROTEST: As a counterstatement to realism, various forms of romanticism have been evident in the literature of this century. Characteristics of romanticism may be seen in the authors' preference of the exotic and fantastic to the ordinary, highly stylized and unusual language over journalistic or conventional narration and dialogue, mythic or superhuman characters, and bizarre or non-conventional plot material. These four main aspects of "neo-romanticism" have many variations, but what they represent as a whole is a kind of protest against the terrible and inescapable reality of modern life. "Romantic" in the largest sense of the word means anti-realistic, and it is a particularly "romantic" notion today for the individual to have precedence over the mass. The works of such authors as Evelyn Waugh, Iris Murdoch, J. D. Salinger, and John Updike (among many others) typify romanticism in this sense. A so-called "cult of sensibility" has grown up in recent years which expresses the individual's private exploration into his isolation and inner developments in opposition to the fixed goals and values of mass society. Since World War II there has been a burgeoning of culture and public awareness of art. It is not unseemly then that readers should be receptive to a revival of literary protest in favor of sensibility.

SOCIAL OUTCASTS: In a manner similar to that of nineteenth-century romanticism which glorified the "noble savage," the neo-romanticists of the twentieth century have glorified the social outcasts. The realists and naturalists have used the urban and rural poor as their vehicles for social protest. In their move away from former tendencies in literature to consider only the aristocracy, they have spoken for the average middle-class citizen and the proletariat. But newer material has been sought by writers of later decades, and the radical result after the war novels has been a growing emphasis on heretofore unexploited types, those whose inherent alienation also served the need for protest. Pitted against the overwhelming odds of his environment are the Negro, the Jew, and the homosexual (man or woman). A more sophisticated and curious reading public has been receptive to these portrayals of alienation whether rendered realistically or romantically. The growth of the social sciences has given substance to the literary presentation of social conflict. The Negro, the Jew, and the homosexual provide symbols for alienated men in the larger sense. The romantic approach to the literature of social protest has been rendered in terms of the grotesque and the absurd. Such writers as Truman Capote, John Horne Burns, and Frederick Buechner have achieved success in the treatment of such figures in essentially a non-realistic way. Such writers have brought protest away from documentation and closer to art. Other artists of protest, such as Alex Comfort, J. P. Donleavy, and Joyce Cary are enraged by the semi-totalitarian order imposed by a society whose values are based on war and death and have created characters of another alienated type—the semi-criminal artist whose regeneration is possible only through social and civil disobedience.

SUMMARY: While the twentieth century has been characterized by a tremendous variety of form and technique and outlook, it is evident that two dominant trends prevail—1) realism, accompanied by naturalism, regionalism, and psychological analysis of character, and 2) romanticism, characterized by fantasy, myth, and innovative style. The development of modern literature has been circumscribed as well as unfettered by two world wars, a world economic depression, the growth of science and technology, the spread of education and mass culture. The tenor of society today as reflected by the arts is a feeling of alienation resulting in man's conscious quest of his place in relation to his environment. Greater freedom of subject matter and manner of presentation have been the outgrowths of this search for identity in an epoch of relative chaos. Optimism, despair, cynicism, violence, abnormality, anger, absurdity, and mysticism, along with revivals of religion, folklore, and myth have characterized the many means employed by writers to achieve the singular end of explaining man's position in the universe. Such variety has produced a degree of confusion among literary scholars, but all seem to agree that literature is far from stagnation, and indeed is as vital as the teeming diversity of the life it reflects.

THE JEW IN LITERATURE

HISTORICAL ATTITUDES: The Jew's place in literature dates as far back as the Old Testament. Hebraic culture is one of the foundations of Western civilization. As the outsider to Christianity, the Jew has always been characterized as the alien—mysterious, fearsome, and unrelenting in his adherence to his faith. During the Middle Ages and the Renaissance, the Jew received unfavorable treatment. (One has only to read Chaucer and Shakespeare.) This was due in part to his unwillingness to be assimilated into Christianity, either as a Catholic or a Protestant, and his preference for social and religious independence, necessitating a rootless, scattered existence rather than a localized, ethnically unified life. Such an existence, coupled with a separateness from fellow Jews, led to the strong defense mechanism manifested in a closed society. Thus, Jews set themselves apart from others and were in turn forced to live in special sections of civilized communities. These sections were known as "ghettos," and here the alien Jews could be confined lest they cause trouble. As a people set apart, the Jews were logical targets for persecution and proved equally interesting subjects for suspicion. Medieval literature is full of unfavorable reference to Jews who were thought to be enemies of the Christian world. The Renaissance did not bring an end to anti-Semitic concepts, and the Jews were still considered outcasts. There have been, of course, numerous Jews who gained fame and favor in the Christian world, but for the most part, anti-Semitic sentiment has prevailed as the mystique of the non-assimilated Jew continued. The wandering of the Jews brought them to the New World, but so far as literature was concerned, Old World attitudes prevailed. As nationalism took precedence over feudal loyalties, the Jew's place in whatever country he resided became more stable, and national loyalty became a new factor in Jewish life. Yet the tendency to ethnocentricity continued, whether self-imposed or forced upon the Jews by the laws that governed him. Consequently, the connotation of Jews as isolated groups became standard in practical living as well as artistic representation. As an inherent defense mechanism against persecution, this sort of voluntary group life perpetuated the mystique of the Jew as a symbol of alienation. The Jew has retained a separate identity, whether as a result of his own clannishness or the restrictions imposed upon him by external pressure.

ASSIMILATION: As the New World beckoned to all peoples seeking freedom and opportunity, many Jews came forth, escaping the persecution of the Old World. Since the nineteenth century, waves of Jewish immigration to the United States have become more noticeable. While considered socially undesirable in many cases, the Jew has always had educational advantages inherent in his background. Historically barred from civil or professional occupations, the Jew has, for the most part, found his livelihood in mercantile areas. As a scattered and geographically fragmented people, Jews have sustained not only a unifying religious tenacity but a sub-culture of folkways as well.

The Jew brought both his religious heritage and folk culture with him to the New World where he hoped to find religious, economic, and social freedom. Ambitious to these ends, the Jew has prospered in America, exchanging hard work for the opportunities made available. Because of the heterogeneity of peoples in America (the so-called "melting-pot" notion), the Jews have become assimilated into American life to a more advanced degree than in Europe. Some interpret this "aculturation" negatively; others react more positively to the connotations of the term "assimilation."

THE MODERN JEW: Optimistic and ambitious for each successive generation, the Jewish immigrants saw their progeny become part of the fabric of American life. While traditionalists bemoaned the loss of former Jewish identity, the modernist thought it a wholesome and essentially beneficial feature of American life. Most Jews, however, remained part of urban society and thus retained a certain clannishness as manifested in the predominantly Jewish neighborhoods of large cities. A few braved it to rural areas for the opportunity to own land—a privilege denied them in the Old World. But business as well as mutual protection and interests kept the Jew largely within the confines of urban areas. The emphasis on family ties was also a strong factor in the localization of Jews. Yet the American penchant for mobility has made for a geographical diffusion of the Jews, and nuclei of Jewish life spread across the North American continent, both in Canada and the United States. Thus, has the Jew established himself in the New World.

SOCIAL CONSCIOUSNESS: Although the overt restrictions of the Old World have been removed, a more subtle process of exclusion has developed in social, economic, and cultural areas. The dominance of the White Anglo-Saxon Protestant has been reflected in American literature. Whatever representation of the Jew existed was noticeable only by inadvertent mention of a "Jewish family" or a typical Jewish name. The emphasis on Jewish identity was ignored as a cultural or artistic factor. However, the Jews maintained a culture of their own as can be seen in the early established and still vital Jewish newspapers and Yiddish theater. The more recently developed Jewish cultural and civic organizations are symptomatic of a so-called

"Jewish Renaissance," an outgrowth of the social consciousness of the earlier decades of this century. The resurgent identity of distinct Hebraic characteristics has its roots in this period.

IMPACT OF WORLD WAR II: Jewish-American consciousness was most profoundly revitalized by the threat of ethnic extinction in Europe during World War II. The atrocities of Hitler's elaborate methods of genocide aroused world attention as well as Jewish-American sympathy. The renewal of old patterns of persecution generated a revival of ancient preoccupations with suffering and alienation. This time, however, the reception of non-Jews was one of sympathetic concern and active participation in countermeasures to Hitler's activities. The image of the totally mortified man was compatible with wartime attitudes, and the Jewish cultural renaissance fostered a momentum that carried Jewish literature beyond its traditional characteristics of nostalgia and defensiveness. The impact of World War II on the public was a greater interest in and receptivity to the Jewish writer who suddenly found his Jewishness at a premium on the literary market. His very alienation was his passport to a substantial place in Gentile culture.

THE JEW AS A SYMBOL: After the flood of war novels, the trend in the literature of the following two decades was toward protest. As we have seen, it took many forms, ranging from the howl of the Beats and the cynicism of the existentialists, to realistic documentation and romantic innovation. Heretofore unexploited as subject matter, the Jew along with the Negro and the homosexual served as symbols of man's alienation from his environment. He represented liberalism and tolerance born of centuries of humiliation. The glorification of his past in relation to modern times can be found in the revival of Jewish lore. The folkways of urban ghetto and rural peasant life have been adapted in the fiction of Sholem Aleichem and Isaac Bashevis Singer. Jewish folk wisdom operating in the contemporary world has been a trademark of Bernard Malamud and Philip Roth. The influence of the theologian-philosopher Martin Buber has found its way into the literary works of today's Jewish writers. This influence is characterized by the revival of Hasidic lore, a conscious effort on man's part to improve interpersonal relations, and a new phase of religious transcendentalism.

There has been criticism leveled at the Jewish writer for over-playing the theme of suffering. And this criticism has a certain validity regarding the oppressiveness of some individual works. However, in respect to the general theme of man in conflict with his environment, the idea of suffering seems infinite, whether presented as the frustration of ipso facto saints, fallible heroes, or the alienated man of sensibility. The current lack of belief in perfection in this life is often transformed by Jewish writers into a herculean attempt to resolve right and wrong. The picaresque Jewish hero of today is a transformation of Tom Jones and Huckleberry Finn into a Holden Caulfield or an Augie March. Saul Bellow's novels have synthesized the conflicts of modern man in terms of a Jewish protagonist who might also be Everyman. Where Bellow's approach has been of a more benevolent sort, the protagonists of Philip Roth have been angry young men. Jewish self-consciousness has manifested itself in the poetry of Stanley Kunitz, Delmore Schwartz, and Karl Shapiro as well as in the dramas of Arthur Miller. It is thought by some critics that the influence of Jewish culture in American letters has become somewhat of a "cult of Jewishness."

SAUL BELLOW'S FICTION

EARLY WORKS: In a lecture delivered in 1963, Saul Bellow stated that "The public realm, as it encroaches on the private, steadily reduces the powers of the individual; but it cannot take away his power to despair, and sometimes he seems to be making the most of that. However, there are several other avenues commonly taken: stoicism, nihilistic anger, and comedy."[1] Presented nineteen years after the publication of Bellow's first novel, these remarks may help direct a discussion of the author's published works.

It has been previously pointed out that the termination of World War II, and its aftermath, left Americans (as well as most other peoples) with an extremely distasteful concept of the direction in which man's values were heading. The result went beyond disenchantment; it extended so far as decadence and nihilism until it came back full-circle. The result was a firm but altered attitude, an acceptance of the alienated individual in a mass society. In literature this alienated being became a new kind of protagonist—not a traditional hero, but an amalgamation of mock and anti-heroism, who conceded absolute rebellion to some form of accommodation.

SIGNS OF THE TIMES: Bellow's two novels of the 1940's showed the temper of the times, but they were more than merely flat portrayals of the spirit of the age. Whereas they moved within the pattern of the period—the movement from alienation to accommodation—Bellow incorporated into their

---

[1] Lecture delivered 21 Jan., 1963 under the auspices of the Gertrude Clarke Whithall Poetry and Literature Fund of the Library of Congress.

characters' personalities some serious exploration into the dilemma of their time in history. *Dangling Man*, published in 1944, has as its protagonist one such typically alienated man whose story bespoke the psychological testimony of a generation. Isolating himself from his family, friends, and works, Joseph discovers the functionlessness and intolerability of his self-imposed freedom. By precipitating his draft-call, he confronts these insoluble problems from within the prison-like walls of a boardinghouse room. But Joseph, searching for some values by which to live, discovers that he is in the prison of himself, and the boardinghouse is only a symbol of his real confines. The steaming windows and tawdry atmosphere are symbolic of the murky outlook created by the limbo between world war and peace in which he is involuntarily cast. Joseph, symbolically isolated from his brethren, is suspended as are his alienated brethren, in an uncertainty too enormous for the individual. He must accommodate it in order to cope, but the price of accommodation is the sacrifice of self-freedom.

Bellow's second novel, *The Victim,* published in 1947, deals with an isolation of a different kind. The protagonist, Asa Leventhal, must cope with the diametric opposition of his own will to action versus his self-imposed sense of impotence and guilt. To fight the battle for life successfully, the middle-class American Jew, as Leventhal suggests, must learn when to disengage himself so as to function. Tormented in a Hamlet-like manner, Leventhal sinks further from action into a contemporary version of loneliness and despair, haunted by the guilt-figures of a dying nephew, a dissipated colleague, and memories of an insane mother.

FEATURES OF STYLE AND THEME: While *The Victim* shows better technical construction than *Dangling Man*, both early works show the intellectual unity and orderly progress which Bellow has followed in his fiction. Before Joseph and Asa are alienated, they are oppressed by the chaos of circumstance and a host of characters crowding down upon them. Short of total subjugation to chaos, distraction, and obligation, the two early protagonists plunge into alienation and move toward an accommodation of those very things that have driven them to their frantic condition. Presenting the two protagonists mock heroically, Bellow demonstrates the impossibility of either conquering the foe. Each has too much rage, despair, and personal comedy to triumph like the traditional romantic hero. The burden is too enormous to be vanquished, but the characters, in their extremely romantic gestures of escape, achieve some degree of reconciliation with their environment.

MIDDLE PERIOD: The mood of the Fifties was somewhat different. It was characterized in the fiction of such writers as J. D. Salinger, William Styron, and Saul Bellow by novels of spiritual quest. Two characteristics of these novels are 1) the self-conscious narrator and 2) the picaresque hero (found in such eighteenth-century novels as *Tom Jones* and *Humphrey Clinker*; modeled after the prototype of picaresque heroes, Don Quixote). The most important work of this period in Bellow's career was *The Adventures of Augie March*, wherein the author presented the episodic self-discovery of a poor, young urban Jew whose demands upon life can be fulfilled only by the answers he provides by his own experience. Augie is caught between the polarities of character and fate, and his adventures provide the novel with its substance—the eventual discrimination between which of the two (character or fate) is the determining factor of one's life. Augie's essential urbanism became a recognized trademark of Bellow's fiction. It is in the clutter, chaos, danger, and enormity of the city that the author's protagonists could move from the naturalistic to the existentialistic, from the alienated to the accommodating. Augie's testament to city life is the affirmation that identifies him as typically Bellovian: "... and I am in a crowd that yields results with much more difficulty and reluctance and am part of it myself." Moreover, that fragment underscores the quest of the Fifties, so well documented and explicated by David Riesman's study, *The Lonely Crowd*. It is in the welter of urban chaos that Augie crystallizes his quest: "Anyway there's too much of everything of this kind, ... too much history and culture to keep track of, too many details, too much news, too much example, too much influence, too many guys who tell you to be as they are, and all this hugeness, abundance, turbulence ... which who is supposed to interpret? Me?"

ACHIEVEMENT AND RECOGNITION: *The Adventures of Augie March* was for Bellow a major achievement. Appearing serially in magazines from 1949 on, it was published complete in 1953 and won the National Book Award for Fiction in 1954. It was hailed by critics for its vitality, richness, originality, and powerful affirmation that life was worth living. What particularly characterized the novel was its defiance of strict concern with form. The author had admittedly "kicked over the traces" and written it "catch as catch can." Yet that very expansive, deliberately self-styled novel signalled the style which was to become recognizable as Bellow's—a bearing of great catalogues of knowledge that simultaneously included and limited clutter. The basis upon which Augie's nascent optimism speaks for a generation is founded upon the assertion of his own character in the teeth of the clutter and chaos. As this personality assumes the nature of reality, the real becomes his fate, which is to go about the business of living and doing despite the vast, confusing determinisms that produce the antagonistic chaos.

TWO LATER NOVELS: In 1956, *Seize the Day* was published. It was Bellow's fourth novel, written under the auspices of a Guggenheim Foundation grant. Its protagonist, Tommy Wilhelm, pitched his battle for life, as Augie March had, in an urban setting. Tommy's struggle was set in New York, but much more than location differentiated this novel from the prize-winner of 1954. It was much shorter and less comprehensive than *The Adventures of Augie March*. It received high acclaim, but not a literary award. Nevertheless, it showed both the consistency and development of Bellow's skill. Tommy Wilhelm, a man enmeshed in a mechanized urban world, is in a desperate phase wherein he can no longer brawl and run. His hidden fantasies serve as a pattern from which evolves the meaning of his last adventure. This crucial adventure must determine whether he can live or must die in a world that has beaten him. It is the vitality of the need to live that motivates his motion toward existence; and in Tommy's revelation, "the consummation of his heart's ultimate need," Bellow reinforces his metaphor of characteristically controlled but definite optimism.

Bellow's fifth novel, *Henderson the Rain King*, was published in 1958. The theme of Eugene Henderson's story is whispered into the protagonist's ear by an African queen: "Grun-to-mo-lani," or "man-want-to-live." Henderson, a Connecticut millionaire, fraught with ambitions and energies, seeks more than his reconciliation with ordinary life. He sees salvation and deliverance through service in hopes of bettering men and freeing them of decay. Bellow's context of chaos for this complex novel is set in teeming, urban Africa and is based somewhat on Neitzsche's philosophy in *Thus Spake Zarathustra*, the laws of King David, and the anti-Freudian psychology of Wilhelm Reich. Henderson learns the practical application of self-transcendence, and thus solves the characteristic problem of all Bellow's heroes to date—opposition to the finite; Henderson is battered by the savages in a symbolic ceremony making him the Rain King. His revelation comes of his struggle to transcend chaos: "This planet has billions of passengers on it, and those were preceded by infinite billions and there are vaster billions to come, and none of these, no, not one, can I hope ever to understand. Never!" The nature of his vision of vast quantities is such that he sees it not as suffocating and depressing, but as something marvelous and full of infinite possibility. It is in the creation of Henderson that Bellow achieves the ultimate success which the early protagonists failed to achieve. He, more than any other, discovers truth and reality in the secret of nature's law—that the *real* is inhumanity and death. The inescapable rhythms of life are man's need to preserve intact the freedom of his personality. That is the crucial necessity of life for Henderson.

RECENT WORK: In the autumn of 1964, Bellow's most recent novel, *Herzog*, arrived on the literary scene and created quite a critical stir. Its public acceptance kept it on the best-seller list, often occupying first place, for many months running. In 1965 it received the National Book Award for Fiction. It was considered by critics Bellow's crowning achievement—a novel of even greater magnitude than *The Adventures of Augie March* (which had won the same award for the author in 1954). While *Herzog* had the same comprehensiveness and self-styled vitality in technique that the earlier prize-winning work had shown, the later novel outstripped its predecessor in richness, style, and character. There were those who assailed it as oppressive in regard to the totality of the protagonist's suffering.

A NEW ARCHETYPE: Moses Herzog, a middle-aged some-time professor, and professional intellectual, suffers, jokes, moans, rages, and charms. He believes himself to be a survivor of his own and the modern world's disasters. He has the answers to everything save the "piercing" questions he cannot refrain from asking. He runs from them to New York, the Berkshires, Chicago, Martha's Vineyard, expressing his "angst" in innumerable letters mentally composed and occasionally half scribbled on anything handy. These letters are to people famous and unknown, living and dead. They express his protest, his insufferable displeasure with the way things have been, are, and will continue to be unless something is done. He cannot act, and when he might, the vitality of his acts either misfires or he flees from them before they bear consequences. The most intelligent, sensitive, mature, and culturally aware of all Bellow's heroes to date, Moses Herzog becomes an archetype of modern civilization. He has paused in the middle of his assorted achievements and failures to take a look at himself. He is appalled, sickened of soul, and wallowing in his neurosis. He bears the magnificent stature of today's serio-comic man who has simultaneously everything and nothing.

The novel carries the full freight of Bellow's intellectual accumulations. He catalogues the public turbulence and private dilemma of the age. The vast quantity of spiritual, historical, moral, sociological, and psychological considerations bearing down upon Moses Herzog are a compendium of the author's past protagonists and anxieties with some new ones added. Once again Bellow is dealing with the idea of the individual self and the mass of the species. Somewhat akin to Henderson, Herzog acknowledges the mystery of mankind as one he personally cannot solve. What he can do, however, is seek effectively self-knowledge and self-perfection. This must be done by action, not inertia and futile protest. No one achieves in a vacuum. No one achieves by playing God outside of himself. His messianic messages for others cease as he, like Candide, symbolically tends to his own garden, and thus becomes his own prophet of action, not mere words. When the novel ends, Moses Herzog's life of renewed action is beginning, and although the "piercing" questions have not been answered in full, they have been faced and debated, for ironically, "At this time he had no messages for anyone. Nothing. Not a single word."

SUMMARY: The novels, short stories, and critical commentary of Saul Bellow over the last twenty years have won for him an important place in American literature. He has been hailed as one of the era's great writers for his thematic depth and comprehensiveness, his style and technique, and for his critical influence. Dealing with questions that plague the modern mind, he has sought the answers through catalogues of all the "isms" and "ologies" of western civilization, achieving an optimism crucial to the survival of modern man's moral and spiritual sensibilities. His writing has shown development and unity in its intellectual and technical progress. He is considered to be one of the most dynamic forces at work in American letters today.

THE ADVENTURES OF AUGIE MARCH

OVERVIEW

THE NOVEL FORM: *The Adventures of Augie March* belongs in part to a genre of literature known as the *picaresque story*, a predecessor of the novel. This type of story developed in sixteenth-century Spain and derives its name from the Spanish word "picaro," meaning rogue. Picaresque stories originally concerned themselves with the escapades of a merry rogue who lived by his wits, and the genre itself was a reaction to romantic or idealized forms of fiction. Episodic in structure and realistic in manner of presentation, these stories were frequently of satirical intent. One of the earliest of the picaresque stories is Cervantes' *Don Quixote* (1605), and another popular example is Le Sage's *Gil Blas* (1715). Variations of the picaresque story were important to the development of the novel as a literary form which came to prominence in eighteenth-century England. Among the novels of this time, those which adhere especially to the picaresque tradition are Defoe's *Robinson Crusoe* (1719) and *Moll Flanders* (1722), Fielding's *Tom Jones* (1749), and Smollett's *Humphrey Clinker* (1771).

The novel of character has its origins in the seventeenth century. The early form was a sketch which represented a way of life or a personality. The first actual novel of character is attributed to Samuel Richardson who wrote *Pamela: or, Virtue Rewarded* (1740). Subsequent novels of character are far too numerous to mention, but it should be noted that this type merged with novels of incident, thus evolving into that sustained work of prose fiction which, despite its innumerable variations, we today simply call the novel. *The Adventures of Augie March* can be seen then as a study in the spiritual picaresque, combining the special elements of novels both of character and incident. However, there is another sort of novel called the *bildungsroman*, a traditional genre in which the picaro's function is especially one of development and deepened consciousness rather than one of merry adventure. The *bildungsroman* is devoted to the growth and development of its main character so that the progression is from illusion to truth, and finally to a recognition of a certain fate.

Mr. Bellow integrates these earlier types of novel forms in *The Adventures of Augie March*. The terminology applied by scholars helps us to identify the ways in which he has amalgamated these specific forms. We see in Augie the importance of character building by means of incidents which stimulate and enlarge upon the somewhat roguish hero's consciousness. We see, as well, the realistic presentation of a somewhat romantic adventurer, the distillation of reality from illusion, and the eventual assertion of an independence from others in a self-created way of life. Modern novels of a young man's spiritual quest are numerous, but significant ones for artistic comparison to *The Adventures of Augie March* are Joyce's *Portrait of the Artist as a Young Man*, Salinger's *Catcher in the Rye,* Updike's *The Centaur*, Styron's *Lie Down in Darkness*, and Farrell's *Studs Lonigan*.

STYLE: The term *style* in literature is usually construed to mean that manner of expression characteristic of a writer. That is to say it pertains to the author's choice and arrangement of words, his figures of speech, the use of rhetorical devices and their effects. At one time, a writer adhered to strict doctrines of decorum by employing a style designated to the subject, occasion, and audience. Although in modern times there has been an easing of this traditional, formal set of rules, most writers do adapt their style to the subject matter and their audience—that is, they are aware of the demands of propriety made by their audience and demanded by their material. Yet the highly individualistic or experimental writer is less apt to be concerned than the traditionalist. It is, however, by means of his style that a writer's reputation grows or diminishes, for discerning readers will demand far more than mere content or form. Style, then, may be considered that special mark of an author's individuality; and the more one reads of a single author, the greater his awareness of the nuances and development of that writer's style. And it is by learning to recognize the existence of style that we gain greater critical insights into literature. Just as Augie claims in the beginning of the novel to "go at things . . . free style," it is perhaps correct to say that Saul Bellow's manner of expression is achieved in a similar way. In commenting on writing the novel, the author claimed to have "kicked over the traces, written catch-as-catch-can." If one examines closely the sentence patterns to be found in *The Adventures of Augie March*, an immediate sense of an informal, anti-literary word grouping can be detected. There is a breaking down of syntax, or a "roughing up of diction," as one critic has phrased it. Here is not that studied smoothness of traditional exposition, nor the esoteric exaggerations of an ultra modernist. What is to be found, rather, is an earthy, natural speech, in keeping with the characters and their respective milieux. In Augie's conversations as well as his narrative passages, there is a continuity of speech pattern indicative of a unified character. His brusque, often ungrammatical language pays homage to the commonplace and the universal, but avoids the overtly vulgar. If there is dialect, it is primarily American. There can be found a few traces of Yiddish influence, and occasional instances where it is necessary to create the speech of a specialized character. The style is one intended primarily to communicate, and its success to this end can be found in the absence of artificiality, but never at the expense of individuality. There is an urgency, an eagerness for telling, in the manner of expression employed by the author. Hence, we find a necessary spilling over of words and conglomerations of ideas not always systematically arranged, but skillfully constructed to support the characterization. The effect of this articulation of immediacy is an intense grasp on the reader's attention, one that sustains involvement. It is worth noting that in later works, especially *Herzog*, the style has become more assured, less slap-dash; but it remains as natural and directly communicative as it is here.

EPISODIC STRUCTURE: As the title implies, the book concerns the adventures of a young man. Each adventure constitutes an episode which has both its individual effect and a cumulative effect in terms of the entire novel. Episodic structure is a very old form, but there have been many innovations added. For instance, there is the flashback, which is a relatively modern technique of re-creating an episode in the past which gives larger significance to the present, used by Bellow quite effectively in *Herzog, Dangling Man*, and *Henderson the Rain King*.

The Adventures of Augie March is made of a progressing series of episodes which have a cumulative effect. Each of Augie's adventures clarifies a specific influence on his development. The cumulative effect is derived by the references to previous adventures and the way each new one is related. As each episode moves Augie along, the adventures and the influences of the people involved become integrated, and in this way the reversal of the character-fate statement is supported by the logic of the progression Augie has followed. The episodes cannot be categorized completely by theme even though there are major emphases of each. For instance, the Einhorn section develops Augie's notion of the mastery of circumstances and prepares him for young manhood in which he will see reversals of fortune as Einhorn himself has. The Mexican episode qualifies Augie's attitude on love, primarily because of his great suffering; but it has greater significance, bringing into focus his alienation by means of the alienated characters who live around the villa in Actala. It also creates a catharsis and re-evaluation period, just as the train-hopping episode did, but it shows a greater maturity, sophistication, and independence on Augie's part in his role as a down-and-outer. The Mexican adventure shows as well his degenerate role in the society of great wealth where he is an alien, a brilliant usurper as he was in the Renling episode. The paralleling of episodes in this way adds to the unity of the novel and affords the reader a comparative basis upon which Augie's development may be better understood. Lastly, episodic structure provides a fluidity of movement for themes and characters as well as opportunities for illustrative examples shown by each episode.

DETAILED ANALYSIS AND COMMENTARY

MAJOR PREMISE—CHAPTER I: When Augie March, the hero and narrator of the novel, immediately introduces himself, he heralds his own singularity and poses an aphorism that will ultimately reverse itself. Boldly he states that he goes at things "free style," in his own way; his premise is that "a man's character is his fate." In the sometimes brawling, sometimes poignant, but always high-spirited adventures that ensue, Augie travels the road from adolescence to self-discovered manhood. And while the weight of life's demands attempt to subjugate him, Augie persists in the exuberant, if occasionally painful, pursuit of self-hood—that totality of being which survives alienation and moves toward accommodation.

COMMENT—Fate: Augie tells us that "A man's character is his fate," according to Heraclitus. The reference is to the Greek philosopher, (540-575 B.C.), one of the earliest metaphysicians, also known as "The Weeping Philosopher." The connotation here is the popular synthesis of Heraclitus that everything is in a state of flux, or more literally, one never steps into the same river twice. An important structural element is to be found in this allusion to metaphysics, for the aphorism (a short, pithy statement of a general truth or doctrine) is to reverse itself at the end of the novel. The term *metaphysics* pertains to that branch of philosophy which includes *ontology*. In a general sense, metaphysics is one of the more abstruse philosophical disciplines which in relation to ontology, treats of the science of being or reality. Ontology itself investigates the nature, essential properties and relations of being; it examines the fundamental causes and properties in things. The thematic structure of the work is given support from this recurrent notion as Augie talks about this fate throughout the novel. For it is Augie's primary concern to investigate the metaphysical or ontological properties of his own being, and thus come to a determination of his fate, although it is to be one that is incomplete, or still in a process of motion. That is precisely why the aphorism reverses itself, for "a man's fate is his character" as Augie eventually decides, and one's fate is not completely determined while life prevails. A fate is a dynamic thing for Augie whose adventures never really end—and the endlessness that he accepts is that quintessential element of his character. Augie says, "All the influences were lined up waiting for me. I was born, and there they were to form me." For Augie, a fate enables one to be a "person and not a function . . . which is a substitution (of fate) of a deeper despair."

GROWING UP—CHAPTERS II-IV: Home for Augie is a matriarchal situation which he shares with his older brother Simon, younger brother George who is mentally retarded, and his passive, husband-deserted mother. The roost is ruled by Grandma Lausch, ostensibly one of the boarders, but in reality a powerful old Russian widow who has taken command of this impoverished Chicago family. Under Grandma's tutelage, the Marches are given economic, social, and educational direction. It is Grandma who sees to it that public charity money is not denied the family even when there is a rare flow of income from other sources. Assisted from the money paid by boarders, the boys are sent out to work at any job which can be secured for them by Grandma's machinations. Despite her subservience and passivity, Mrs. March is the love force of the household. Overworked, she is subjugated by the force of others' passions, but she is never under appreciated, nor is her emotional capacity unfelt when, infrequently, it is totally asserted in grief.

The Marches are Jews, living in a shabby but respectable section of Chicago in the nineteen-twenties. Aside from the early lessons of anti-Semitism learned in the street, the family's religion is not given major emphasis. It remains, however, a point of consciousness and identification in a social and abstractly ethnic sense for Augie throughout the novel. Those aspects of Jewishness that are implicitly stressed are the family's devotion to one-another, the ambition and capacity for hard work exhibited by the boys for their own and the family's betterment, and a certain emotional pitch which is often a characteristic attributed to Jewish people. But the real religion of the Marches is that of sustaining life, keeping things going in spite of adverse circumstances. To this end, Augie and Simon dedicate themselves with a robustness and vitality often attributed to Bellow's characters.

Unprotected from the reality of life's demands, the March boys are endowed with both the resilience to survive the mishaps of circumstance and the energy to seek again and again realization of the goals for which they strive. The March boys are not free from minor temptation offered by the plentiful crime opportunities in the Chicago of that era. According to their code of ethics, a degree of right gain may be derived from brief encounters with wrong. In this period of Chicago's history, it is often difficult to tell just who is and who is not criminally connected. The most important thing is that the boys contribute to the family's support, and it is Grandma Lausch who arranges for their early employment. Simon spends summers in his teens as a resort bellhop. Augie is farmed out to relatives named Coblin to do odd jobs. It is here that he sees a somewhat more affluent life which is offered to him on the conditional basis that he surrender a portion of his individuality. And as he will not do so in this instance, neither will he do so as subsequent similar opportunities arise. The summer with the Coblins marks for Augie the point at which the significant influences of people outside his home are noted and chronicled throughout the novel: the philosophers, big-shots, sufferers, crooks, lunatics, and genuine heroes.

As Augie's world expands, he experiences life beyond the pale of Grandma Lausch's commanding influence. Simon becomes the financial mainstay of the family while Augie finishes high school. Slowly it becomes Simon who replaces Grandma as the head of the household—but not without a struggle that deals Mama a severe and permanent emotional blow. This signifies, as well, the inevitable deterioration of Grandma's authority, and reveals to Augie a propensity toward power he had never before recognized in his older brother. The upshot of these developments is the institutionalization of George. The result is a gradual weakening of family life as it had been known up to now. Simon undertakes the task of securing employment for Augie, who endures a variety of jobs with singularly little talent for success. Augie feels the weight of Simon's contempt and fierceness as he had once experienced the same things from Grandma Lausch. But, characteristically, the younger boy takes it in stride, merely noting, not yet judging.

COMMENT—Narrator: *The Adventures of Augie March* follows the pattern of many of the so-called "quest novels

1704331

of the Fifties." One of the techniques employed by the authors of these novels of spiritual quest was the use of the first-person narrator. The rhetorical effect of a first-person narrator is often misleading, for it causes many readers to presuppose the validity of everything. In other words, only one point of view is fully substantiated. The function of rhetoric is to persuade; to this end the first-person narrator is most successful. A direct dialogue is set up between the speaker and the reader. When other characters disagree with or criticize the narrator, the reader is apt to rationalize for or defend the narrator who has engaged his sympathy. In his book, *The Rhetoric of Fiction*, Wayne C. Booth speaks of the self-conscious narrator whose rhetoric makes his own consciousness that of the reader as well. Booth also remarks that Saul Bellow's novels require great subtlety on the reader's part because of the questionable reliability of the narrator. In defense of his technique, a comment by the author here is useful: "The intention of the writer, therefore, is to hold the reader to a sense of the weight of each action. The writer cannot be sure that his million (readers) will view the matter as he does. He therefore tries to define an audience. By assuming what it is that all men ought to be able to understand and agree upon, he creates a kind of humanity, a version of it composed of hopes and realities in proportions that vary as his degree of optimism. . . . The writer must find enduring intuitions of what things are real and what things are important. His business is with these enduring intuitions which have the power to recognize occasions of suffering or occasions of happiness, in spite of all distortions and blearing." The student will be better able to appreciate the technique of a first-person narrator if he keeps in mind both Booth's and Bellow's remarks. For, if the narrator is only partially reliable, then it is to the student's advantage to look for significant voices among other characters who may illuminate Augie more objectively. At one point, Augie remarks that he is going to say more about others than about himself so that we may determine the influences upon him. There are many such clues employed by Bellow in Augie's narration so that the reader can avoid becoming overly involved with the narrator.

THE FIRST HERO—CHAPTERS V-VII: Augie notes that William Einhorn, a cripple whose capacity for life had in no way been diminished by his affliction, was "the first superior man" he ever knew. Einhorn, part of a politically and financially influential family, employs Augie in the capacity of a junior factotum for the few years immediately preceding and following the Great Crash. It is from Einhorn that Augie receives a first-hand view of an individual's mastery over life's details. The influence that Einhorn exerts can be traced throughout most of the novel as it is subsequently incorporated into the evolving philosophy of young March even after the aura of the crippled mastermind has grown somewhat dull by the light of wider knowledge. From Augie's relationship with Einhorn and his relatives come vast quantities of characters and experiences—all registering, all being amalgamated into the youth's conscious reality of growing up.

COMMENT—Heroic Vitalism: A term that has occurred frequently in modern literature is that of "heroic vitalism." What it really means, as the words imply, is a vital sense of life coupled with the heroic intentions of a character. Many of Mr. Bellow's figures are heroic vitalists in spite of the anti-heroic outcome. Augie certainly qualifies, as do Grandma Lausch, Einhorn, Mimi Villars, Mintouchian, and Frazer. That is to say, each of these characters represents the concept of a superman (in the Nietzchean sense) whether fully realized in life or not. They have a drive to overcome the limitations of their lives, and are able to accomplish much toward their goals. However, heroic vitalism in a character does not preclude an anti-heroic destiny, for it does not mean that a crucial compromise won't be made for success. What matters is that the quality of heroic vitalism prevents absolute defeat. The anti-heroic outcome for the characters keeps the superman concept within the bounds of reality. Whereas false supermen, such as Joe Gorman the criminal and Robey the millionaire are defeated, the realistic supermen (heroic vitalists), Einhorn, Simon, Augie, Mimi, Mintouchian, Padilla, and Frazer—succeed by an even exchange with life, blow for blow.

INDIRECTION—CHAPTER VII: While Einhorn's influence is notably far-reaching, it does not provide Augie with a real direction. Still wanting a greater clarity of things, detecting a longing to know just where his life is leading, Augie muses, "Crusoe, alone with nature, under heaven, had a busy, complicated time of it with the unhuman itself, and I am in a crowd that yields results with much more difficulty and reluctance and am part of it myself." The administration at home is now completely surrendered to Simon, and Grandma Lausch retires herself to an old-age home. The brief period of financial ease is not fated to endure, for lurking in the all too near future is the Crash of 1929. With employment practically unavailable, flirtations with minor league crime were experiences that both March boys had, but only until honest remunerative work could be found. It is Einhorn who set Augie straight on the dangers of illegal activities. And it is in this instance that Augie distinguishes between the relative and the absolute criminality of one's life. Even the rites of manhood presented to Augie as Einhorn's high school graduation gift signify the subsequent schism between the elder man's attitude toward women and what is to become Augie's. From this phase of his life Augie has achieved that nascent sense of self which scents but craves more recognizable manifestations of his ultimate personage.

COMMENT—Philosophy: An important aspect of the *bildungsroman* is that the central figure must grow in his consciousness, his awareness of, and relationship to his environment. Either he moves closer toward or further from his starting point in his spiritual quest. In order for the reader to perceive the character's development in thinking, the author must provide opportunities in which thoughts can be shown as part of the growing process of the major figure. The reader can perceive only limited aspects of the characters' development in the actions (and reactions) taking place in each episode. Augie's actual philosophical growth is expressed in two ways: 1.) in his "deep" conversations with other characters and 2.) in his dialogue with the reader in which he comments on himself. Frequently in this novel, the reader will notice a few lines of philosophical musings at the beginning of each chapter. Sometimes they are about life in general; at other times they pertain specifically to Augie. These passages of philosophical illumination are not hidden or designed to be abstruse. They are as directly presented as the author's style. Remember, Augie is eager to TELL, for in relating his adventures, he arrives at a synthesis of his own beliefs. It is interesting, however, to note the way in which the author selects those characters who will act as sounding boards for his philosophy. A character of lesser importance is usually the one to whom Augie addresses his great ideas and discoveries about life. Two examples of this are Augie's conversations with Kayo Obermark and Clem Tambrow as his philosophy of life is becoming clearer to him near the end of the novel. Major characters are usually too involved in exerting their influence on Augie for long philosophical discourses to take place. However, with certain ones—Einhorn, Simon, Mimi Villars, Padilla, and Mintouchian, for example—certain kernels of Augie's philosophy occur in conversations to be developed later in his reflective dialogues with the reader. A philosophical exposition usually serves to elaborate upon or explicate the themes condensed within the action of the novel. However, *The Adventures of Augie March* is a novel of a genre that demands philosophical clarification—both for character and reader.

THE RENLINGS—CHAPTER VIII: For a substantial portion of the Depression, things go well for Augie and Simon. Both are employed and taking night-courses at the city college. Mama is losing her eyesight, but the young men are able to afford a housekeeper to look after their home. Both brotherly affections and competition motivate their actions and their development. It is significant, however, to mention that growing aloofness and distance which occurs during these years which distills their individuality and separates their eventual destinies. When Augie is given a chance to move ahead socially, financially, and culturally by meeting the Renlings, a childless older couple, he allows the opportunity to enfold him in a new phase of development. As Mr. Renling's business assistant and Mrs. Renling's protege, Augie learns much about himself in relation to this way of life. While the trappings of this class appeal to his newly-discovered vanity, the one drawback he finds to accepting the permanence of it as offered by the Renlings is himself. His individualism cannot accept a role not self-created, nor is his curiosity to know life yet sated. He must go on at the forfeiture of a grandeur that may never return. He must still become that new person demanded by every situation until he meets his "axial lines"—those singular guideposts of existence which validate one's own version of life. Perhaps it is his failure to conquer by love the niece of a millionaire that causes his awareness that it is time to move on. The actual rift with the Renlings, however, is the result of their efforts to gain too strong a hold on him.

> **COMMENT—World of Chaos:** Related to Augie's disengagement is the world of chaos from which he desires to distill a sense of order. To this end he must necessarily remove himself, if only intellectually, while continuing to participate on a modified basis. He flees, essentially, from the demands of other people. Everyone seems to want Augie to subscribe to a value system of theirs, not his own. The complex pressures create a weight from which Augie wishes to extricate himself. Several critics have applied the sociologist David Riesman's theory of the "inner" and "other-directed" man as propounded in his book, *The Lonely Crowd.* This thesis treated the condition of post-World War II society, and it illuminated the various facets of the new individual's chances for opposing the new mass with its collective goals, values, and satisfactions. In a comment made about *The Adventures of Augie March*, Mr. Bellow said, "I do not believe that the human capacity to feel or do can really have dwindled or that the quality of the human has degenerated. I rather think people appear smaller because society has become so immense. Hugest of all are the fears that surround us. These are what make it hard for us to determine our proper size and the importance of all our deeds."

It is just this welter of mass society that produces the chaos from which Augie must disengage himself in order to determine his place in a self-created order of things. We see the substantiation of this motif in the vast quantities of characters in the novel who constantly shove their values at Augie. This thematic climax occurs during Augie's job for the millionaire, Robey, when in a conversation with Clem Tambrow, a fellow boarder at the Owens', the individuality struggle becomes crystallized. Augie tells Clem, "And then you go and pile on top of that more advice and information. . . . Any way, there's too much of everything of this kind . . . too much history and culture to keep track of, too many details, too much news, too much example, too much influence, too many guys who tell you to be as they are, and all this hugeness, abundance, turbulence. . . ." Having followed Augie thus far in the novel toward this gigantic accumulation of ideas, notions, philosophies, influences, advice, we can identify the thematic import of this outburst as the climax of Augie's opposition to the mass society which pulls him into its chaotic multiplicity of direction. This sort of indecisiveness has been an important condition of man's existence since World War II and is a theme treated notably in Mr. Bellow's first novel, *Dangling Man*, and his two most recent novels, *Henderson the Rain King* and *Herzog*.

THE SKIDS—CHAPTER IX: Fearing the suffocation of an adopted embrace, Augie returns to Evanston rather than to Chicago. He visits Grandma Lausch and is appalled to find this once seemingly indestructible person senile and rapidly deteriorating with very little time left to live. From his recently superior position in life, Augie now travels in the opposite direction. Fortune reverses itself, dealing out to the young man a series of brief, unpleasant, and unsuccessful jobs. He learns how to live on a frayed shoestring—one ready to snap at any moment. But Augie discovers that if you move fast enough, your weight never lingers long enough to weaken those few solid threads: "It was not only for me that being moored wasn't permitted; there was a general motion, as of people driven from angles and corners into the open, by places being valueless and inhospitable to them." A criminal enterprise of running immigrants over the Canadian border to the United States is the next abortive attempt at making enough money to contribute to his mother's support. The result of this misadventure is a three-week interlude of train-hopping in an effort to return to Chicago. Being a hobo brings to Augie's cache of experience new despair and startling insight into the condition of humanity.

COMMENT—Alienation: Augie's alienation from his surroundings is not as complete nor as tragic as that of Stephen Dedalus (in Joyce's *Portrait of the Artist as a Young Man*) or Holden Caulfield (in Salinger's *Catcher in the Rye*). For Augie, it is a matter of disengagement bespeaking his opposition to being caught in a disappointed life or another person's scheme for living. He holds out, like Stephen and Holden, for a destiny or fate worthy of his talents and ideals. But he is never as isolated from his family and social connections as the characters of Joyce and Salinger. Augie's is a modified alienation; he has neither Holden's psychological inability nor Stephen's excrutiating sensitivity that would keep him from some form of vital participation in life. Only during his period of suffering and convalescence in Mexico is Augie relatively isolated from life. But he cannot escape into that totality of alienation illustrated by Holden or Stephen. For even at his most removed, old connections manifest themselves (former Chicago friends miraculously appear in Mexico) to accentuate his disengagement and to thrust him back into motion and activity. Augie never categorically rejects his environment nor his associations. His disengagement is illustrated by his continual acceptance of the validity of other people's lives, even if they are not suitable models for his own. It is in his lack of commitment to anything in particular throughout most of the novel from which we derive a sense of Augie's alienation. However, most alienated characters suffer extensively from loss of innocence or the failure of an heroic ideal. Not so Augie. His alienation and suffering are the results of attempted commitment until the problem reaches its anti-climactic solution in his acceptance of a permanent lack of commitment and the role of a continual fate-seeker.

FAMILY CRISIS—CHAPTER X: Upon his return to Chicago, Augie finds his mother now blind, dispossessed and living with friends. In a frantic attempt to save a romance, Simon has wrought destruction upon the household and himself. It is several months before he and Augie see each other, for Simon's disgrace and despair have embittered him too much to allow him to face his younger brother. It is at this point that Augie realizes his spiritual superiority over Simon and comes to his first overt judgment of his brother. Again it is Einhorn who intercedes with disaster on behalf of Augie and finds him a job so that Mrs. March will be supported. But Einhorn's influence is waning, for time and experience have put a noticeable distance between his and Augie's view of things. Luckily for Augie, he meets a former city college classmate, Padilla, a Mexican, now a scholarship student at the university in math and physics. It is through Padilla that Augie's life turns to books— as a means of both financial and intellectual gain. With Padilla as his mentor now, Augie achieves a new form of solidity, if not a permanent one. For Padilla's detachment does not create in Augie that fear of encroachment which other influential relationships have insidiously attached to them.

RECONCILIATION—CHAPTERS XI-XIV: In the meantime, Simon has been re-working the pieces of his exploded existence, and simultaneously hardening into the man he is going to be. The reconciliation between the brothers is characterized by Simon's permanent hardness and effrontery and Augie's sentimental gladness. It is Simon's plan to marry a rich girl and become a wealthy man using his intended bride's family money as a starter with a fortune of his own to be built on it. He plans also to undertake the tutelage of Augie, and to move the younger man from his barefoot, book-surrounded, semi-student existence to a position of subordinate wealth and importance. Simon's new master plan goes into successful operation. Augie's fortunes rise as he enters his brother's coal business. With difficulty, the younger brother manages to remain at college a while longer. However, Simon's plans for Augie include heavy social responsibilities, and studies are soon foregone in pursuit of Simon's wife's cousin, a young lady of even greater wealth than Augie's sister-in-law. Yet young March remains in his garret-quarters, thus retaining his individuality in those friendships within the milieu of students vaguely affiliated with the university. These are the individuals who are later to give him a permanent nucleus of operative values. Augie is living and learning much during this second rise to upper-middle class comfort, but his somewhat Bohemian life creates the circumstances by which he will extricate himself from his closest flirtation with a permanence not of his own making.

COMMENT—Anti-Heroism: Still another important motif, related to the themes of alienation and chaos, is that of anti-heroism. In the traditional connotation, the hero is one who overcomes his opponent because his is endowed with those noble qualities which make his conquest appropriate. The anti-hero, or mock-hero, originating in the picaresque story, is someone who achieves his goal, but not in the fullest sense; he may have to make a singular compromise. Moreover, the anti-hero is not a particularly noble person. It is often circumstance that engenders his modified triumph. The anti-heroic motif occurs throughout *The Adventures of Augie March*. Pitted in a crucial manner against something, each character of importance fails somewhat to achieve his goal in totality. There is some weakening, some compromise to be made, some flaw in the outcome. In a sense, the anti-heroic motif is a device of the realistic writer. For Bellow it seems to be a method by which a degree of romanticism is introduced thematically. For each major character exhibits an unflinching strength in support of his vision, and fails to fully acknowledge defeat when it is imminent. For example, Einhorn's drive for power is successful in a limited fashion, and while he admits that on the 30th day of every month he knows he has been beaten, he yet exists in a self-created environment that enables him to be a superman. Iggy, the man who initially seeks to console and regenerate Augie in Mexico, is another type of anti-hero. He has been defeated by his ex-wife but persists in retaining a relationship with her even though it is degrading. His eventual reunion with her is even more unheroic. Yet it is nonetheless a realistic sort of passive heroism in which his qualifications are determined more by circumstance than inherent zeal. Mintouchian and Mimi Villars, along with Padilla and Stella are anti-heroic. They succeed in the sense that they have survived some brutalities of life and reached their goals. Their actions may even be construed as genuinely heroic. However, their successes have left them embittered or compromised in attitude. That is, they represent the relative success of the "disappointed life" which Augie fears for himself. Simon and Augie exemplify the anti-heroic in that they, too, ultimately accommodate themselves to their fates. Simon achieves his much sought wealth, but at a price. Moreover, it is made clear throughout his development in the novel that Simon is capable of such compromises in order to fulfill his acquisitive ambitions. For Augie, the anti-heroic motif is related to the foibles of his nature which keep him from achieving the ultimate state of *being*. Rather, we find him, as the novel ends accommodated to a continuing state of *becoming*. The thematic intent of Mr. Bellow's anti-heroic portrayals of character is to illustrate his notion of the diminished stature of today's fictional characters. They represent the "kleine menschele" (little man) existing in a society too immense to give the individual a sense of significance. The theme of "moha," opposition to the finite, is an important aspect of Mr. Bellow's fiction. His characters must struggle against the limitations of a crowding, demanding world in order to achieve individuality, which the author equates with an unlimited or infinite sense of the self and its capacity for achieving life. The motif of anti-heroism illustrates the individual's accommodation to life, which is never a total victory, but a relative one. Or, as Kayo Obermark tells Augie, everyone accrues bitterness in his choice, because, as Augie reasons, "to arrive at the chosen thing needs courage, because it's intense, and intensity is what the feeble humanity of us can't take for long."

MEXICAN INTERLUDE—CHAPTERS XV-XX: As Simon's hold over Augie grows stronger, fate devises a series of incidents and misunderstandings which will terminate, if rather disastrously, Augie's bondage. This time, however, Simon's rage is consummate, and Augie is cut off from work, money, and his intended fiancée. Far from crushed, except by Simon's inflexibility, Augie wanders briefly and finds himself a union organizer in a rough, post-Depression situation. Undaunted, he takes his knocks as they come until a promise made during the Renling episode is fulfilled. The millionaire's other niece has come to claim Augie as she said she would even though it was her sister that had so infatuated the Renling's former protege. Thea is enroute to Mexico to await a divorce decree. Augie gladly gives up the career of bruises and batters as union organizer and surrenders his fate to Thea with whom he has fallen deeply in love after a few luxurious days in Chicago. With Thea's seemingly limitless funds, the two set off for Mexico in opulence and style. Once at their destination, it is Thea's plan to train an eagle for falconry and sell the story and pictures of this as well as other hunting and sporting endeavors to magazines. While love, money, and success in hunting and photography last, Augie and Thea enjoy an unparalleled idyll. Soon, however, little failures of the project befall them, creating disillusionment and finally disaster. Augie is seriously injured, creating a heaviness of time which the couple try to alleviate by mingling with what would be considered the jet-set of the 1930's—the rich and those attached to them—the somehow universally displaced who wander from one resort to another seeking relief from their boredom and frustrated existence. But rather than soothing the growing discontent of the couple, these misfits accentuate it, and the result is the colossal rejection and desertion of Augie by the admittedly neurotic and permanently dissatisfied Thea.

COMMENT—Intellectual References: An important technique of a writer is the references to things beyond the immediate character or situation which supply, by metaphorical inference, the comparison he wishes to imply. It is a technique of condensation, but its effect is one of diffusing the impact of a point of view. In the broadest sense, Mr. Bellow's references imply his adherence to the tenets of humanism. That is to say the author subscribes to those humanistic principles originating in the Renaissance which became the foundations of the Enlightenment. Humanism in this sense is man's ability to triumph over the supernatural or otherwise predetermined obstacles of his destiny. Man is a creature of free will rather than one of predestination. As such, the humanists believed that man is his own messiah. Mr. Bellow pits his characters

against the suffocating determinations of the modern world
—its complexity, its demands, its chaos. By allusion to
historical figures from intellectual, literary, and political
history, the author supports the notion of the humanism
by which his characters live. Of course, one of the perjor-
ative facets of Mr. Bellow's humanism is that his references often pertain to superman figures modeled after
Machiavelli and Nietzsche.

In general, however, it may be said that Mr. Bellow is
seeking in his heroic models of all types to substantiate
the personalist heroes of his own fiction who must be as-
sertive of the self that modern society disallows. (One critic purports the theory that this exercise of personality
stems from a tradition of Yiddish literature called "dos
kleine menschele." Marcus Klein feels that it is this little
man from the ghetto of Eastern Europe whose survival
amidst the omnipresent perils lies in his strenuous assertion of personality.) Two such specific references to great
personalities that occur in *The Adventures of Augie
March* are Alcibiades and Bolingbroke. It is in his relationship with Einhorn that Augie alludes to Alcibiades.
The interpretation here comes from Shakespeare's *Timon
of Athens* in which Alcibiades is the brilliant but trai-
torous Athenian rebel who overcomes the resistance of the
city supported by the misanthropic Timon. Einhorn may
be considered as the Timon figure and Augie representative of Alcibiades. In another interpretation, Alcibiades
was a favored pupil of Socrates. Both interpretations relate
to Augie's role as an Alcibiades in his brilliance and estrangement from his fellow creatures. The reference to
Bolingbroke is also from Shakespeare. Characterized in
the plays *Richard II* and *Henry IV* (Parts 1 and 2), Bolingbroke, Duke of Hertford, is the brilliant usurper. Exiled
son of John of Gaunt, Bolingbroke succeeded in his usurpation of the English throne by conspiring against Richard
II, and despite his faulty title to the monarchy, became
the successor known as Henry VI who created a ruling
structure that was passed on to his heirs. Augie is called
"Bolingbroke" by Iggy Blaikie, one of the group sojourning in Mexico. The nickname alludes not only to Au-

gie's relationship with Thea, but to his characteristically successful usurpation of a role. However, there is much irony in the nickname; in this particular episode, Augie meets his most colossal disaster, and so the name becomes hateful to the defeated aspirant. But since this group of people is better cast as something they *might* have been, Iggy persists in calling Augie Bolingbroke, but in an affectionate way. For it is Iggy who offers moral support to Augie in his crisis following Thea's departure.

THE WAY BACK—CHAPTER XXI: Desolate, ill, and reduced to pauperism, Augie remains in Mexico in a futile wait for word from Thea. Fate provides him with a companion—the least dissipated of the hotel crowd—who offers sympathy, advice, and a kind of strength to the disconsolate and shattered Augie. Eventually, a former Chicago cohort appears in Mexico attached to the staff of a great exiled revolutionary. Moved by Augie's plight, he finds a benefactor for the still convalescing fellow-Chicagoan. After a period of months, Augie returns to his hometown and on the way stops to see his brother George at the institution. He is greatly moved by this hapless young man's capacity to live in a relative state of dignity with his fate. Upon his return to Chicago, Augie is reunited with his brother Simon, who is as eager to show the younger man his own success as to help him toward success of his very own design. Rather than live entirely on Simon's support, Augie takes a job working for a rather unhinged millionaire bent on writing a book, a guide to man's happiness based on the works of all the greatest thinkers of history. The appeal of the job to Augie lies in its opportunity for vast quantities of reading which will supplement his resumed university studies and nourish his appetite for knowledge. But the would-be author's madness becomes too great a demand, and Augie leaves the job.

COMMENT—Sense of Life: A theme which occurs in *The Adventures of Augie March* reappears in the phrase, "grun-to-molani," or "man want to live," in the later work, *Henderson the Rain King*. The earlier work does not illustrate this vital sense of life as powerfully as the later one, but the motif is nonetheless an important part of the work. While the primary theme is Augie's determination to create an order for himself out of chaos, the intense desire for life itself, for achieving "true joy" is a relevant and necessary secondary theme. It accompanies the motif of heroic vitalism in its insistence on the value of being actively alive. In a Whitmanesque manner, Mr. Bellow demonstrates this sense of life in Augie's celebration of himself and his growing affirmation of selfhood. The drive within Augie to live as himself and no one else is related to "moha"; for to be one's very self, an individual must avoid the determinisms that represent the finite. The infinite self is the one that escapes the chaos, that achieves simplicity and order, and finds operative truths and values. The self's fulfillment is not completed by Augie's "going everywhere" at the conclusion of the novel, rather his fulfillment is seen in terms of the drive to have come through the intermediate stages which preceded his selfhood. The vital sense of life shows in Augie's personality which exerts an influence on the outcome of things equal to that exerted by his adventures. It is apparent in Augie's resilience after defeat, and in his refusal to accept substitutes for the reality of living. Hope and belief as opposed to inertia and despair are other illustrations of Mr. Bellow's sense of life.

It is here that the anti-heroic motif gains greater meaning. For no one can remain untouched or unaltered by life, particularly those who exert their personality as intensely as Augie and other Bellow protagonists. Thus driven by their individuality, the characters assert personality over circumstance and give full expression to their exuberant selves, driven by a vitality that brings to the author's fiction a brilliant affirmation of life itself. This is effectively brought out at the end of the novel as Augie bursts out laughing on a trek across the raw wintry landscape of Normandy: "That's the 'animal ridens' in me, the laughing creature, forever rising up . . . or is it the laugh at nature —including eternity—that thinks it can win over us and the power of hope. Nah! nah; I think. It never will."

AUGIE'S VISION—CHAPTER XXII: With Simon married and settled in his hard-won luxury, and Mama now in a home for the blind, Augie is free to live in the surroundings he has always found the most pleasant—back at the rooming house that he had once shared with the university crowd. His contacts as substantial as ever, Augie does not lack for companionship. Yet he is not the same man he was before the Mexican episode, and is in fact still recuperating from the physical and emotional strife it produced. However, he is in the process of achieving a goal that only he has set for himself; attending the university in preparation for teaching. His elementary school practice-teaching is a thoroughly rewarding experience, one which leads him to a definitive pronouncement of his vision. And this is to marry, buy property, and set up a home-school for children from institutions who would be taught by himself and his wife. For, as Augie explains, "All I want is something of my own, and bethink myself . . . I'd never loan myself to any other guy's scheme."

COMMENT—Self Identification: *The Adventures of Augie March* is a large and complex novel incorporating many motifs or themes. We usually define *theme* (interchangeable in modern criticism with the word *motif*) as an abstract concept embodied in the structure and imagery of a work of imaginative (or nondidactic) literature. The theme or motif of a work applies to a recurrent character, incident, or concept. It is not necessary that a work have only a single theme; there may be a major motif and several minor but closely related ones. Such is the case with *The Adventures of Augie March*. It might be stated that the major theme of this novel is the order of the self and its value in a crowded, demanding, chaotic world. This motif is crystallized in Augie's concept of "axial lines": "Truth, love, peace, bounty, usefulness, harmony! And all noise and grates, distortion, chatter, distraction, effort, superfluity, passed off like something unreal." But around that location and ordering of self, are many other concepts, important enough in their own right to be considered minor themes of the novel.

AUGIE'S FATE—CHAPTERS XXIII-XXVI: Circumstance again tickles Augie's transitory quiescence. This time it is World War II. Because of the injuries sustained in Mexico, he is rejected by the Army and Navy, but is accepted by the Merchant Marine. Always desirous of being involved in the most crucial action of life's experience, Augie eagerly pursues his military service which takes him to New York and the Brooklyn Navy Yard. Living in Brooklyn is a former acquaintance from Mexico, a woman who is very similar in philosophy to Augie and with whom he finds substantial love upon which to fulfill his dream of marriage. Before they are married, Stella introduces Augie to the last mentor he is to encounter in the novel—the lawyer, Mintouchian. He prepares Augie for that ultimate accommodation to life which he will have to make. Mintouchian says "It is better to die what you are than to live a stranger forever." And so Augie enters a state more of being than becoming as he marries Stella and fulfills his military service. The last bout with circumstance occurs in a shipwreck from which Augie barely escapes. His escape reaffirms the life principle. Adrift in a lifeboat with Hymie Bateshaw, a demented scientific genius, Augie first argues and then fights desperately for the life that has to be lived by the whole person not just the intellect devoid of heart and soul. We leave Augie after the War residing in Paris with his wife, and conducting a black market operation for Mintouchian. His vision of the home-school is still there, but only for a while. The aphorism with which he opened the novel is now reversed: "Well, then it is obvious that this fate, or what he [man] settles for, is also his character." Admittedly he is still becoming, he has not yet reached the point of total being, but he is convinced that those "axial lines" can be found. "Look at me," Augie says, "going everywhere!"

COMMENT—Sense of Self: Clem Tambrow makes reference to Augie's "nobility syndrome" by accusing him of an inability to adjust to reality. "You want there should be Man, with capital M, with great stature . . . I know what you want . . . O King David! O Plutarch and Seneca! O chivalry! . . . O Don Giovanni . . . O godlike man! . . . You're going to ruin yourself ignoring the reality principle and trying to cheer up the dirty scene." While Augie persists a bit longer in his comparative references to historical heroes, he realizes that his imitative mock-heroics make traditional heroics absurd. For the individual must be his own hero, not a false hero modeled after some admirable or detestable great personage. His one minor brush with the exiled living revolutionary hero, Trotsky, awakens him to an aspect of Clem's "reality principle," but at the time of the occurrence he does not realize it. He is not quite finished with his dreams of becoming a godlike man. He would be a Jesus-figure in his home-school in that he would "suffer the little children to come unto him." Although he carefully considers the plan, he does not urgently press for its realization. The immediacy of the war dispels his personal notions for a while. When in the Merchant Marine he met Hymie Bateshaw, a somewhat demented scientist who would attempt to create life in a laboratory, he realized the horror of man's actual attempt at playing God. For Augie the consummate realization of his place in the order of things occurs in Paris where he tells the reader, "to tell the truth, I'm good an' tired of all these big personalities, destiny molders, and heavy-water brains, Machiavellis and wizard-evildoers, big-wheels and imposers-upon, absolutists. After Bateshaw . . . I took an oath of unsusceptibility." It is a renunciation of his great catalogue of heroes in preference to the assertion of his own personality, through which he achieves the right to exist.

COMMENT—Autobiography: The trend of readers today is to make each reading experience into a witch-hunt for the author's autobiographical disclosures. The psychological orientation of our times provides the assumed privilege of such speculation. Few authors can escape the influence of their own experiences. Or, as Mr. Bellow phrased it in answer to a question about the autobiographical references in his novels, "Every writer borrows from himself what he needs." We can see in *The Adventures of Augie March* certain obvious aspects of the author's own life: the Chicago setting, the Merchant Marine service, and a general philosophy which seems to run its varied course through Mr. Bellow's novels thus indicating a portrayal of his own thoughts on the human condition. However, novels are works of prose fiction, and the concealments of the author's own self are as subtle as the pseudo-psychiatrist-reader believes they are obvious. One may wish to believe that *The Adventures of Augie March* is an autobiographical chronicle of Mr. Bellow's attainment of manhood, or that *Herzog* is Mr. Bellow's self-portrait of a middle-aged intellectual in crisis. And indeed the novels may have many referents in the author's personal life and thought. However, the sophisticated reader will accept them as all novels are primarily intended—as works of art which speak, if successfully forged by the author, to all men on their level of sensibility. It is true that many novels of to-day are obviously autobiographical and presented as "apologias" (defenses) for the writers' lives. But it would be difficult to construe Mr. Bellow's fiction as such. Rather, one should accept the view that most critics take of his works: that they investigate modern man's position in a chaotic world with the identifiable personal touch of the author in the issues he raises, the expression of characters, and his inimitable style.

CHARACTER ANALYSES

AUGIE: Reminiscent of the picaresque hero, Chicago-born Augie March is engaged in numerous adventures which constitute a spiritual quest. The son of a loving but ineffectual mother and an absent father, Augie is easily influenced by the people he encounters, but he eventually rejects the system of any other person, preferring to let his fate be the determinant of his character. An engaging personality, good looks, a vital sense of life, and a susceptibility to circumstance are among his more marked characteristics. Going at things "free style" is his "modus operandi." He is capable of both toughness and sentimentality. He is earnest, but not especially naive; rather he is curious to see how things will turn out, and at times things become calamitous for this picaresque pilgrim. He is capable of being both an altruist and a bush league crook. His affability makes him generally well-liked, and he can be a charmer with women. He is often considered by others to be someone they might like to adopt (Einhorn, the Renlings, Thea, and others adopt him to some extent). Augie's is at first an heroic vision, one that takes its models from great figures of history—both good and bad: Machiavelli, King David, Napoleon, Nietzsche, Socrates, John Dillinger, and Julius Caesar, among others.

Augie starts upon his quest with his so-called "purest ideas" intact. In a way he resembles Huckleberry Finn, for Augie displays a singular reluctance to be determined. His elusiveness, combined with his grand (and sometimes grandiose) assertion of personality, constitutes a kind of freedom from the chaos and demands of a burdensome world. His gesture of escape is essentially romantic, but his eventual accommodation to life signifies his realistic destiny. Given to mock-heroics throughout his running, brawling adventures, he functions to point out the absurdity of the traditional hero in the modern world. His greatest show of courage can be seen in the vigorous exercise of personality. By this is meant the courage to be himself, preserved and intact. The result is a freedom closely akin to alienation. The freedom from commitment, either by defiance or evasion, becomes a moral liability with which Augie must eventually come to terms. All he asks is to be saved from a "disappointed life." It is Augie's compulsive exertion of personality that saves him from embitterment, but not from making some sort of realistic, operative compromise. The bouyant spirit that is Augie's to the last page speaks out jauntily, "Look at me going everywhere." This sort of virtuosity is frequently a characteristic of the author's protagonists, and it is a trait which often constitutes the very essence of their freedom. It might be said that it is Augie's virtuosity which is in conflict with his imperative need to love; that is, he must choose between love and its relative loss of self or a totally independent fate and its accompanying alienation. While the major action of the book concerns Augie, he is to a large extent outside the action. As the first-person narrator, he tells the readers that the book will be less about himself than those people and incidents which became his fate. In this way, Augie's role is one of disengagement even though the novel provides for his full development as a character. We can trace him by phases throughout his many episodic adventures: from his non-judging, ever-aware boyhood, through his financial, occupational, and romantic ups-and-downs, to his sophisticated, judgment-skilled manhood. The fate he settles for or admits to is a kind of restless impermanence, a continual striving toward a state of *being* rather than that of *becoming*. In other words, he succeeds in his opposition to "moha" or the finite. His quest then ends on a dubious note: "I may well be a flop at this line of endeavor. Columbus too thought he was a flop, probably, when they sent him back in chains. Which didn't prove there was no America." And Augie has not proved nor disproved that life cannot or will not subjugate him; rather he has only avoided subjugation thus far. In a sense, then, Augie has accomplished what he set out to do, for his adventures never really end. But he has failed too, in preserving intact his existence. He must keep on—"going everywhere."

SIMON: Augie's older brother Simon has a multiple function in the novel. He serves as an influence and a parallel to the major figure, and as such, he is the closest object of comparison and contrast to Augie. His influence as the head of the family is an important feature of his role in the novel. Since this function comes early in the work, it augurs the shape his values will take as he develops. He is always concerned with money as a source of power, and power as an ultimate achievement. He is much more capable of toughness and cruelty than Augie because he has as his singular characteristic a fierce pride rather than the exuberant and forceful personality of his younger brother. He is far less concerned with sensibility than with tactics. He is the politician, the Machiavelli of the family, whereas Augie might be considered the wandering diplomat. His tenderness is always sheathed in wrath, whereas Augie's manifests itself in sentiment. Despite the closeness in which Simon and Augie live or work, there is always a distance between them. This distance does not preclude genuine love, nor does it foster jealousy or contempt. It simply exists as a factor of delineation and makes allowances for objectivity in the relationship. Simon's devotion to Augie is both generous and selfish. He really wants to help his younger brother but is frequently exasperated by Augie's disengagement from his favors which shows in the junior March's lack of overt appreciation and frequent resistance. Simon's selfish motivation to help Augie is his desire to be a permanent influence, winning Augie over to his view of things. This can be seen in the jobs he arranges for Augie and especially in the relationship he encourages between his brother and his wife's cousin (Lucy Magnus). Eventually Simon recognizes Augie's independence and offers help without strings attached. This is important because it reinforces Augie's position in the novel. In contrast to Augie's destiny, Simon exemplifies the bitterness with which the success of compromise is accompanied and the "disappointed life" that ensues. While Simon achieves a more secure grasp on life, conversely, it assumes an equally strong grip on him such that he can never let go for a split second or he might lose too many of his hard-won, ever-demanding goals. In this sense, he represents the Machiavellian figure whose philosophy is that it is better to be feared than loved. The major point of contrast between the fates of the two March brothers is that Augie gives himself over to love in his marriage to Stella, whereas Simon's marriage to Charlotte is a duty-bound pact in which he has consigned his freedom to his wife in return for her wealth. Augie considers this "his [Simon's] mismanaged effort to live . . . to live and not die." And this, according to Augie, is a source of shame.

GRANDMA LAUSCH: The first of the major influences on Augie, Grandma Lausch is one of the female versions of heroic vitalism in the novel. She is the widow of a Russian merchant from Odessa whose own children, having outgrown their need if not their love for her, support her residence with the Marches. Her need to influence a family has led her to the role she plays in her adopted family—that of a matriarch. In the absence of a father, the March boys as well as the passive mother profit more than they occasionally suffer at the potent will of the older woman. She possesses certain distinctive qualities of the exiled Russian Jew: 1) she is not religious in the traditional sense, having witnessed the pogroms (mass murders of Jews in Russia) and lost her faith in the benevolence of a benevolent deity; 2) she is shrewd and conniving in matters of survival; 3) she is superstitious in her maintenance of certain old world, semi-religious rituals and customs in matters of the household, and the fate of people with hereditary flaws; 4) she is cultured and sophisticated and maintains a venerable image among her fellow emigres. In the March household, her will is indomitable and her word is supreme. She is honored and attended, spoiled, loved, and feared. She, too, is a Machiavellian in this sense. Were it not for Grandma Lausch, Augie and Simon would not have such drive and ambition, nor the capacity for such hard work as they exhibit, for their mother is far too passive to wield the necessary authority. Grandma Lausch is impossible to satisfy, exercising her autocracy on the local tradesmen, neighbors, and cronies, as well as the family. Hers is a firm belief in retribution whether administered by fate or by herself. Grandma Lausch is not warm or affectionate, but her love for the March family can be seen in her concern for their welfare and the great lengths to which she goes to keep them from going under. Undoubtedly, she is motivated to this dedication to the Marches by need and pride more than love, but she serves them well as the iron-willed "grande dame." Presented by Augie as an influential factor in his life, it is in keeping with his development that her position of power should give way to the others (first Simon within the household and then Einhorn from without) and that her inevitable failure as an omnipotent figure should occur. However, she retains, as do the rest of the influential characters, a singular mark on his development.

EINHORN: William Einhorn, described by Augie as "the first superior man I knew" is another profoundly influential factor in the life of the young protagonist. He, like Grandma Lausch (and later Mintouchian), is another Machiavellian figure—always plotting, master-minding, commanding and teaching by object lessons. Augie compares him to Julius Caesar in modern greatness of character, and Louis XIV in autocracy. Ironically, Einhorn is created by the author as a paralytic, with dead limbs save for his hands. In this sense he is modeled after the maimed supermen of history such as Moses, Mahomet, and Oedipus, among others. His power is an overcompensating machine of mind and spirit. He is constantly in action, either relating to the family's many business and political ventures, or involving his personal business of vast correspondence, file-collecting, fact-gathering, amateur writing, and finance-managing. Moreover, Einhorn is something of a ladies' man. Happily married to a woman of unquestioned devotion to him, he manages to subjugate his secretaries in a quasi-sexual manner, thus achieving for himself a doting harem in which he revels busily and autocratically. On the other hand, Einhorn has his weak spot, and that is his preoccupation with death, which for him, is an inescapable ghoul loitering always in the background of his relatively paranoiac imagination. Augie is Einhorn's factotum: butler, chauffeur, companion, assistant, et al. Or, considered in another light, Augie plays the role of the wandering prodigy and Einhorn that of the spiritual father. (This sort of relationship is a traditional one in literature and can be found in many variations, a most similar example being Stephen Dedalus and Leopold Bloom in James Joyce's *Ulysses*.) It is Einhorn who instills the basic principles of manhood in Augie who reveres him and acknowledges his shortcomings as well. When the Depression wipes out Einhorn's finances, Augie must be let go, but not abandoned. And it is Einhorn to whom the young man is to return after each adventure and through whom many a crisis will be distilled. But Einhorn's influence wanes as do all the others', precipitated by instances in which his mentor has been too hard on people Augie cares for. There is also the awareness in Augie that he and Einhorn are of different generations and experiences. However, it is a realization of a different sort which causes Augie's concept of Einhorn to diminish, and that is that the now white-haired old autocrat, like Grandma Lausch, is not indomitable.

THEA: First encountered as the sister of the girl with whom Augie falls in love while sojourning at a resort as Mrs. Renling's protege/companion, Thea Fenchel is to play a role of major importance in the life of our protaganist. Heir to a fortune, Thea vies with her sister for Augie's love, only to be rejected as he is by Esther (Fenchel). Promising to reappear in his life, Thea takes Augie's gentlemanly refusal of her favors with apparent calm and dignified determination. When she does again appear in the novel, it is after a hiatus of several years. This time, Augie finds her irresistible, and following his desires without a second thought for the consequences, he accompanies Thea to Mexico where she is bound to await her divorce decree.

Thea's wealth is not her only asset. She is beautiful, sensuous, energetic, intriguing, and sophisticated. Her background has provided her with a wide range of activities, travels, and interests that place her in what we today might call the "jet-set" category. Augie's availability makes him a more than likely candidate for an adventure with someone like Thea. Initially, her plan is to make herself financially independent by means of a photographic career devoted to subjects of unusual sports related to hunting. Provided with the knowledge and accoutrements of sophisticated sports usually available to only the wealthy, Thea's first project involves training an eagle to go after lizards. Augie undertakes the project with her and proves an able but disconcerting assistant. It is in relation to her projects that the more undesirable aspects of her personality manifest themselves: her basic problem is one of being permanently discontent, and her tremendous need for fulfillment cannot be satisfied by any disciplined activity. Initial failure, as with the eaglet "Caligula" (named for the Roman Emperor Gaius Caesar, 37-41 AD, a cruel tyrant given to epilepsy and incest) precludes re-structuring and renewed endeavor: this parallels her relationship with Augie. She has sought love's perfection with him in an idyllic situation that must sooner or later come to grips with the failures and successes of reality. His one not-so-innocent mission of chivalry with another woman (Stella, whom he eventually marries) is the culmination of the many growing failures of the relationship. Thea will not accept the possibility of making amends, for Augie's weakness, like the eaglet's, cannot be corrected nor tolerated.

While Thea's love is lethal, it does provide Augie with a context for learning. His failure in romantic love with Thea makes him all the more determined to try again—if not with her, then eventually with someone else. The disastrous end of the affair provides a pivotal point in his development, for it is the last time he lends himself to anyone without assuming his share of the control. The recuperation from this adventure is commensurate with the intensity of the love they shared. As for Thea, her neurotic restlessness drives her to far distant places and people. One assumes that disaster attends her kind of love regardless of its object. But the effect of this relationship turns out eventually to be advantageous for Augie in future love relationships.

MAMA: A passive and careworn woman, Mama's major characteristics are great gentleness and an ability to sustain love beyond the proportion of the grief it has given her. Her role in life is one of submissiveness—to the husband (a questionable matter of legalization) that has abandoned her and her three sons, to the indomitable Grandma Lausch who assumes the authority of the household, and to all the other demands made upon her by her children, boarders, and neighbors. The drudgery of her life is somewhat oppressive, mitigated only by the love she derives from her children, qualified by their own short-comings as it may be. Mama is saved from being a pathetic figure by the guilelessness of her devotion to serving others. She is suspected by Augie of being one whose susceptibility to love precludes any natural inclination to self-preservation, and hence she serves as a model to him of passive love's eternal retribution. He frequently mentions his own susceptibility to love as an inheritance from his mother.

MIMI VILLARS: An important influence on Augie is his friendship with another character of heroic vitality—Mimi Villars. Like Einhorn and Grandma Lausch, Mimi is a law unto herself, but more important, she operates within the context of Augie's generation and his society. Mimi is "in opposition" to what she considers wrong with the world. But her method of "opposing" is vital, active, and toughened from experience, whereas Augie's is relatively passive, circumstantial, and based on intuition for the larger part of the novel. What Augie learns from Mimi is that everyone is out to ensnare another person into sharing his fate. This knowledge is a confirmation of what Augie had instinctively felt but had never consciously given a name. Mimi's view of life is far rougher than Augie's ever becomes, but he recognizes in her a vast repository of opposition that he can in part apply to his own methods. He and Mimi share a friendship of great honesty, respect, and mutual aid throughout most of the novel. Mimi is as despotic in her amorous relationships as Grandma Lausch was domestically. She is as treacherous an adversary as she is loyal in friendship. The result of her "opposition" in comparison to Augie's, is that Mimi acquires bitterness in her life, whereas Augie does not. She is, nonetheless, an important heroic figure in the novel.

CHARLOTTE: After a disastrous love affair, Simon arranges to meet and marry Charlotte Magnus, daughter of an exceedingly well-to-do family in Chicago. Charlotte, like Simon, is a self-possessed individual who knows what she wants and is willing to pay the price of attaining it. Her love for Simon is a forceful one which exerts as much power over him as her money. Without her, she knows that Simon could never acquire the wealth and status that marriage to her will bring. Her family considers

Simon a "good investment," for his driving ambition will bring dividends. Charlotte is as ruthless in her way as Simon is in his. For while she early submits to his power over her love for him, she triumphs ultimately in achieving control. Having permitted him the use of her love and wealth in order to acquire his material goals, she has also suffered from the knowledge that his love exists in the romances he has outside of marriage. Infinitely secure in the respectability of her position as his wife, as well as in the knowledge of its essential necessity to his financial and social situation, Charlotte exacts her retribution in her capacity as the shrew he has helped her become. Charlotte and Simon are for Augie a singular example of people who "settle" for an existence inclusive of everything save happiness, which for Augie, is equated wtih love and whatever is paramount to making it work.

PADILLA: Manny Padilla is another important influence on Augie. An ambitious Mexican immigrant, Padilla has scraped an existence out of dire poverty and hard work to gain his place in life. Employing means on whichever side of legality aided him toward his goal, he has supported himself through the Depression while studying biology and physics at night. Manny is a wizard in his chosen subjects and finds in academics a chance to succeed in life. He is the main source of encouragement to Augie intellectually and academically. It is he who instigates Augie's romance with intellectualism. He provides Augie with moral support and a second, significant start at studying. But Manny represents more than academic encouragement in the development of the protagonist. Padilla is something of an existentialist with a cool indifference to circumstance and an unflinching discipline toward his goal. He has learned to simplify his life. He tries to instill these things in Augie and succeeds to some extent. He is a loyal friend and mentor during this phase of Augie's development and his influence can be seen from then on throughout the novel.

MINTOUCHIAN: An interesting admixture of Padilla's existentialism and Einhorn's Machiavellianism, Mintouchian is a successful New York lawyer whom Augie meets during his service in the Merchant Marine. Reminiscent of Einhorn, Mintouchian is a conniver, fact-gatherer, and expert arranger of things, people, and information. Like Padilla, he knows the truth about life and has carved out for himself a guilt-free existence suited to his needs. He is a hard, sharp-minded man of affairs of worldly and intellectual learning. Augie calls him a "monument of a person . . . who persistently arises before me with life counsels and illumination." His remarks on marriage are hard, un-romantic, and sound. Although Augie resents the marital advice at the time when it is given, it nonetheless later stands him in good stead as a basis for coping with certain aspects of his marriage. The most important thing Mintouchian tells Augie is that "It is better to die what you are than to live a stranger forever." In his own dualistic way, the crafty lawyer lives this advice for himself. He does not preach his particulars to Augie, but offers only friendship without the customary strings attached. One feels that it is the crucial function of Mintouchian in the novel to remove those last remaining cobwebs of debilitating naivete and altruism from Augie's developing philosophy. The result is for Augie a clear view of the way things are and an approach to making them the way he wishes them to be. It is the influence of Mintouchian that gives Augie a notion of his own power to control himself within circumstance if not always to conquer or escape it.

STELLA: Augie meets Stella, a beautiful, intriguing young wanderer, in Mexico where she has followed a man who was to have helped her in her career as an actress. Involved in intrigue and danger, Stella flees Mexico aided by Augie. It is at this time that he commits the indiscretion that destroys his relationship with Thea. Cloaked in half-truths and confusion, Stella's background is never entirely clarified. When Augie meets Stella again a few years later, it is in New York while he is in the Merchant Marine. It is Stella who introduces him to Mintouchian. Stella's role in the novel is not so much one of cause, but of effect. She is the reality of love as well as the reconstruction of romance. The basic emphasis of Augie's successful marriage to Stella is love, which for Augie is the only true course in life. Theirs is neither an idyll nor an "arrangement"; it is a marriage that accommodates both. Augie admits that neither of them is the most honest type in the world. Stella is still involved in aspects of intrigue that attend her job as a minor film actress. Augie is still "going everywhere" in search of his "axial lines." What accounts for their success in marriage is the ability to love each other mutually as well as individually to protect their private visions.

GEORGIE: Born an idiot, Georgie March is Augie's younger brother. Removed to an institution by the prodding of Grandma Lausch, his departure signals the beginning of the deterioration of family life. It was Georgie who had held the family together in the sense that one of the brothers—usually Augie—had to be at home to relieve Mama of attending him. Georgie serves another important function in respect to Augie. Years later, while visiting Georgie at an institution where he has learned the rudimentary skills of shoemaking, Augie recognizes the inherent dignity in his idiot brother who has successfully met and coped with a fate he could not control. In this sense, he puts to shame both Augie and a number of other characters in the novel who cannot meet their destinies without the loss of some dignity or a violent struggle.

FRAZER: As a graduate assistant in political science, Hooker Frazer is first met in the novel as Mimi Villars' man. Frazer is characterized as a man of ideas. Having been expelled from the Communist Party, Frazer then is reunited by the Bolsheviks. Frazer is a revolutionary idealist whose detachment from any debilitating involvement in human affairs is his chief characteristic. He is somewhat of an historical visionary, a prophet of civilization's future. He is neither an altruist nor a Machiavellian. Frazer is a man of theories he is not afraid to put into practice. He is characteristic of many American intellectuals between World War I and II whose disillusionment with America found outlets in revolutionary activity. To Augie he represents the intellectual version of rugged individualism, and his counsels are to be heeded for their objective worth. The trouble with Frazer as far as Augie is concerned, is that his ideas are for masses of humanity, not for individuals. However, Augie does inherit from Frazer a sense of objectivity, finding in him admirable qualities of intellectual dynamism and auguries of ultimate greatness.

LUCY: Charlotte's cousin, Lucy Magnus, is the young lady selected by Simon to be Augie's future wife. Wealthier than her cousin, Lucy attracts Augie in a passive, somewhat secondary way, for she has neither the good looks nor the strong personality traits he most admires, although she is reasonably attractive and pleasant. For Augie, marriage to her might have resulted in an outcome similar to that of Simon and Charlotte's relationship. Augie allows circumstance to intervene and Lucy passes out of his life without defenses, excuses, or much regret. Save for a point of honor which he lets slide, Augie is genuinely relieved if temporarily discomfited by the end of the relationship with Lucy which was a game in which he felt obligated to Simon to play.

JIMMY KLEIN, JOE GORMAN, DINGBAT: These three represent the varying degrees of criminal experience for Augie. (It should be noted here that book stealing under Padilla's influence is a different sort of illegal activity which Augie differentiates from actual crime.) As a pal of Augie's youth, Jimmy Klein is singled out by Grandma Lausch as a reprobate and an undesirable. During a stint of Christmas employment, Augie and Jimmy embezzle a sum of money and are caught. The lesson is learned, but the aura of Jimmy's criminality lingers in Augie's mind. Ironically it is Jimmy who as a store detective protects Augie from being arrested for stealing books. Dingbat is a relative (stepbrother) of Einhorn. Without being a hoodlum, Dingbat affects the gangster type of that era and leads an irregular life related to Einhorn's pool-room and the activities of an ex-fighter whom he promotes. Joe Gorman provides Augie's closest brush with the law in a scheme involving stolen cars and illegal immigration activities. Augie narrowly misses the fate of Joe, who is caught and pistol-whipped by the police and eventually jailed. Thankful that Joe never squeals on him, Augie ponders the bloody, miserable visage of Joe in the police car which looms like a specter for many years to come.

CLEM TAMBROW and KAYO OBERMARK: Although cast in the novel with different personalities, these two characters have a similar function in their relationships with Augie. Both gain significance in his life as the novel progresses from the point at which Augie re-enters the university. Owens' boarding house also figures largely in their relationship with Augie, as their significance is an outgrowth of this phase of his life. The similarities between Clem and Kayo are that 1.) both have relatively stable values and goals, 2.) both are less curious about life and therefore less romantic figures than Augie, 3.) neither one is an especially heroic type, 4.) each one cautions Augie to accept the principles of reality and the finite limitations of one's life, and 5.) both function as a "sounding board" for Augie as his philosophy matures. In a sense, their characterizations take on a specific significance through their conversations with Augie; otherwise they would be relatively unimportant other than as ballast for the more vivid, heroically-cast types in the novel. Of the two, it is Clem whose insight into Augie gives him precedence over Kayo as a character.

SUMMARY OF CHARACTERS: As this is a long and complex novel, it contains a large cast of characters who represent different aspects of Augie's development. It should be noted that for the most part, all of the characters are essentially urban, and in general, they represent two economic strata—the rich and the poor, or the privileged and the underprivileged. Taken *in toto*, they represent the crowded world with its multiple demands and tensions which shape Augie's development. As individuals, they become isolated personalities with whom Augie has some significant interchange of ideas.

CRITICAL REACTION TO
THE ADVENTURES OF AUGIE MARCH

EARLY PRAISE: When *The Adventures of Augie March* was first published as a novel in 1953, (portions of it had appeared in magazines while it was in progress), it attracted much attention and praise. Major critics, such as Alfred Kazin, Robert Penn Warren, and Anthony West, considered it a major achievement in fiction on the basis of its originality of style as well as the importance of what it had to say. It stood out from the author's previous works, *Dangling Man* (1944) and *The Victim* (1947) by virtue not only of its size and magnitude of subject, but because it represented a greater stylistic achievement than the two earlier novels. Moreover, the work was considered a major statement of a generation and an important contribution to contemporary thought. Mr. Bellow received the National Book Award for Fiction in 1954 for this novel—further testimony to the critical favor it received. *The Adventures of Augie March* stood as the author's major achievement until the publication of *Herzog* in 1964. At that time, most critics felt that Mr. Bellow had surpassed his earlier success in style and in subject. (Further critical comparisons will be made in the subsequent discussion of *Herzog*.) However, as the author continued to produce novels, scholars became more aware of his importance to American fiction. It is in view of his subsequent development that a change in attitude toward the 1953 novel has occurred.

RE-EXAMINATION: John W. Aldridge, critic, scholar, and lecturer, was one of the first to re-examine Mr. Bellow's award-winning novel. In his book, *In Search of Heresy* (1956), Mr. Aldridge devotes a chapter to a comparative study of three novels of the spiritual picaresque: *The Catcher in the Rye, Lie Down in Darkness*, and *The Adventures of Augie March*. In the critic's opinion all three novels have suffered from magnified public acclaim, and all three works fall short of true merit in that they lack the drama, textural richness, and complexity necessary to works with the philosophical implications they purport. More specifically in relation to the novel with which we are concerned, Mr. Aldridge points out that there is a conflict between the picaresque tradition of Augie's adventures and the exposition of Augie's character that weakens the novel. Another point of criticism is that the social scene, so important to this type of novel, becomes inspecific, and that the vividly drawn characters around Augie become isolated, over-described personalities. Lastly, this critic maintains that Augie's progression in the novel becomes superficially motivated as his purpose or problem loses dramatic significance and intensity because of his inability to form a commitment. Thus, Augie's problem is basically inadequacy as a character in relation to the metaphysical complexities involved.

Marcus Klein, a critic who has devoted much time and study to the works of Saul Bellow, sees *The Adventures of Augie March* as part of the author's systematic exploration of the problems faced by post-World War II writers. Mr. Klein discusses all of the author's works within the framework of his thesis—the movement of modern man (of the 1950's) from alienation to accommodation, related in large part to the sociological theories of David Reisman. Commenting on all of Mr. Bellow's novels (exclusive of *Herzog*), Mr. Klein points out certain strengths and weaknesses as the author's work has developed. In relation to the novel with which we are concerned, this critic agrees with Mr. Aldridge that Augie's lack of commitment to anything specific makes his adventures seemingly endless, and that because of this, the character lacks the moral liability for the issues inherent in the novel. It is in the weight of the chaos of Augie's world that the novel bogs down, despite its bouyant aspects of vividly created personalities. It is the inconclusiveness of the novel that Mr. Klein sees as its flaw. However, he points out that among the many redeeming features is that one strong implication of hope perfected by the characterization of Augie as a mock-hero. Moreover, throughout the novels Mr. Klein has discussed, he sees Mr. Bellow as a crucial investigator of the human condition—a significant enough role even if he does not find the solutions.

ESSAY QUESTIONS AND ANSWERS

1. What is meant by the statement that Augie moves from alienation to accommodation?

ANSWER: The novel is concerned with the attempt of its protagonist, Augie March, to overcome the chaos and burdensome demands that seem to be crowding in upon him. These demands may be seen as the attempts of people to make others share their fate (as Mimi Villars puts it). Alienation then, for Augie, is a sense of separateness, a deliberate effort on his part to remain uncommitted to anyone else's scheme. The motion of the novel is created by the episodic structure in which Augie moves through his adventures always participating within the sphere of someone else's influence, but in actuality retaining his avowed aloofness. However, he cannot remain untouched by life, considering the magnitude of his experiences. Both successful and disastrous participations leave their marks on him. The farther he moves into an alienated state, the more the insignificance of his own individuality bothers him. His failure with Thea marks the point at which alienation becomes a threat of permanent isolation. Never does Augie feel compelled to "belong," for he has too much "opposition" in him. Rather, he accommodates life by coming to terms with the very aspects of the chaotic existence he has sought to escape. For Augie, the method of accommodation is never totally fulfilled. It begins with his vision of "axial lines" which signify essentially a form of harmonious order bringing peace to the striving individual. We leave Augie in a condition of *becoming* rather than *being*. That is to say, he has had his moment of truth, has become reconciled to the greater part of his fate by successfully asserting his personality into the weltering demands of life and accepting or accommodating himself to the outcome. Hence, he is still "going everywhere" as the novel ends, but has become accommodated to that restlessness and energetic activity that is his fate.

2. What function do the super-heroic character types serve in the novels of Saul Bellow?

ANSWER: We know from the outset that Augie's fate is the result of the influences that were waiting for him. As we read further we recognize the influences as certain types of people modeled after the philosophies of Machiavelli and Nietzsche. These people, such as Grandma Lausch, Einhorn, Mintouchian, Padilla, and Mimi Villars, are those who have successfully refused to become the obedient slaves of society. They are models of opposition even greater than Augie's own brand of it. Further allusions and references to historical personalities indicate the heroic bent of Augie's mind. In short, the heroic influences on Augie are models of personal self-assertion. However, the contexts of their opposition are never the same as Augie's. For the protagonist of this novel is not a superman. He has too strong a moral concept to permit his success as a Machiavelli or a Nietzsche. Augie is "dos kleine menschele," or the little man of today who opposes, but does not overcome, his role—his one specialized function in a finite world. The super-heroic types whom Augie knows personally or those in the history of Western thought that he refers to have an ironic function in the novel. They represent the futility and absurdity of traditional heroics in the modern world. They illuminate Augie's position as a mock-hero of talent, bravado, and earnestness, but never successful pretension. It is these heroic types who ironically induce Augie to become himself.

3. *The Adventures of Augie March* is a large and complex work, involving a multiplicity of themes and structural devices. How does Saul Bellow manage to unify the novel?

ANSWER: A frequent restatement of the major theme is one of the ways in which the author holds his novel together. The basic motivation of the protagonist is his desire not to be overcome by the weight of modern life. To this extent, his moving serially through the many episodes without remaining in the conditions set up by any of them is a structural device which adds unity. The advice offered by the influential characters about retaining one's freedom is another method of thematic unification. Augie's "opposition" tactics in comparison and contrast to those of his heroes is an important supporting device for the notion of personal heroism and its limitations. The notion of a disappointed life as evidenced by other characters in the novel provides the necessary antithesis for controlling the elements of heroic vitalism which might otherwise overweight the work. The character of Augie, himself, is the most important unifying device, for it is through him that structure and theme are ultimately distilled.

4. Saul Bellow is considered one of the leading authors of today, and is usually singled out for the impact he has made on the reputation of Jewish writers in this country. What might be said of the Jewish aspects of *The Adventures of Augie March*?

ANSWER: Aside from the direct references to Augie's religious background and the fact that Bellow makes a statement about the relative unimportance placed on religion within the family, there are many other instances of the use of elements of Jewish culture in the novel. From time to time there are Yiddish words and phrases occurring throughout the text, mostly in conversations. However, there are many more subtle aspects of Jewish influence to be found if one looks carefully. For example, certain traits, such as close family ties, strongly ambitious tendencies, social discomfort, and "in-group" connections are among those indirect implications of the novel's Jewish background. Then, too, there is the idea of the little man "dos kleine menschele" of the ghetto imperiled by a hostile world outside which is used by the author as a referent for the personalist hero represented by Augie and other vivid, self-assertive characters. This theme, however, is cleverly adapted by Mr. Bellow to make Augie a mock-hero of the modern world which threatens the individual. The successful integration of Jewish themes and contemporary considerations on a universal scale is what makes this novel a more valuable and important work than one of more limited ethnic concerns. For it is in the broadening of specifics into general applicability that the author creates a work of interest to all people, because it lends a greater sense of objectivity to an otherwise highly subjective, and thus limited, topic. It is felt by some social critics today that the problems of being in the minority (such as those a Jew, Negro, or homosexual faces) have become the problems of the individual within the mass. Hence, the integration of specifically Jewish themes and those of a general nature reveals a "zeitgeist" thesis of this novel and help it to stand as a major work of modern American fiction.

5. Augie's goal is a difficult one to achieve and he never really attains complete fulfillment within the novel. Does this mean that the author is basically pessimistic in outlook?

ANSWER: On the contrary, Saul Bellow is usually considered a very optimistic writer. His protagonists are frequently given to visions of love for humanity, tempered only by the circumstances of their lives or characters which may preclude the carrying out of these altruistic visions. Augie is one such character whose vision of love for life is what helps him to pull out of his alienated condition and seek his "axial lines." There are contrasting characters in the novel whose cynicism or pessimism cause them to settle for far less than the life for which Augie strives. However, the extent to which Augie would live in a self-created Utopia must be tempered by the realities of modern life as well as those of his own character. Therefore, he must continue to strive for fulfillment even as the novel ends, for the clutter and distraction of modern life cannot be totally, permanently overcome except by death and it is in keeping with Augie's restless nature to keep on striving. For what Augie learns is that his brand of boisterous, self-assertive freedom is a dynamic thing until one acquires true wisdom and enters his full state of being. Augie's acceptance of a vastly improved state of becoming with optimism for his eventual fulfillment is all that can be expected of a realistic modern "hero" such as he is. The conclusion of the novel affirms both life and self, but leaves room for greater achievements to come.

HERZOG

GENERAL ANALYSIS

Moses E. Herzog, Ph.D., a man of our time, has reached, in his middle forties, a season of discontent. Through a number of processes, he overcomes a psychological crisis resulting most immediately from his second divorce. Itinerant professor and potentially an intellectual of some merit, he devotes this briefly frantic phase of his life to working through his own problems of the past and present. Through the character of Herzog, the author presents the exposition of a state of being by creating a pastiche of the fragile fragments of the life of a displaced person of our civilization. A man of intellect and sensibility, Herzog flounders from place to place—New York, Martha's Vineyard, Chicago, and western Massachusetts—writing unmailed letters to varieties of people, protesting not only his own condition but that of a contemporary man driven to the edge of sense by circumstances for which he is questionably responsible. Herzog's intensified self-awareness generates the consternation he himself feels, drawing both sympathy and contempt from his multitudinous acquaintances. Deeply preoccupied, he is only partially aware of the external world whose balm and chafe bring him to the "piercing" questions of our generation.

Like many other Bellovian protagonists, Herzog is herded like a frenzied animal into a self-created cage which becomes, not the exile of peace he had hoped for, but an arena of confrontation with those same "piercing" questions whose elusive answers may provide a rationale for living. Herzog's most desperate need is to maintain his sanity by regaining control of the unwieldy chaos which has alienated him from himself and the world. An essential element of this great need is the function of communication. Hence, the letters, which in effect are a collective SOS. We learn from the fragmented flashbacks, the circumstances of the past, and are made to feel, by means of the fragments of the present, the intensity with which Herzog is ferreting out of the clutter a life of significance. Groaning, suffering, and malediction are not Herzog's only methods of ratiocination; he can laugh at himself and the absurdity of others with humor and generosity. He can be both tolerant and intolerant of the events and people who have brought him to this frantic moment which sustains itself throughout the entire novel. Herzog's moment is one in which he is socially, emotionally, and financially "out of it," but his intellect and earthy wisdom (of strongly Yiddish flavor) preserve his vitality and serve to reconstitute his temporarily maimed zest for living. Herzog's crisis is, in a sense, a vindication of the right of contemporary man to be eternally human despite the cruel capriciousness of the circumstances under which he lives.

Married the first time to a plain, mid-western Jewish girl (Daisy), Herzog left that marriage as the result of inexplicable pressures. This divorce, hard-won, from his first ex-wife is still a rational one, and the child of this marriage, a son, Marco, has been able to spend much pleasant time with his father. After drifting through a few love-affairs, notably one with a Japanese art student (Sono Oguki), Herzog succumbed to his second wife, Madeleine Pontritter, an extraordinary young woman of beauty, intellect, and neurosis resulting from an ultra-bohemian upbringing. For all its pathos and diabolism, the marriage to Mady was a satisfying one by virtue of its intensity. For it is just this intensity of which Herzog is deprived after the divorce. The more bizarre aspects of his marriage to Madeleine are recounted and re-suffered by Herzog as he gropes his way through the dilemma of the novel.

The second divorce is one of the main points of the novel's focus. The psychological, intellectual, emotional and financial demands of the marriage are a magnified synthesis of the problems of many modern marriages. The second Herzog marriage involved two incompatibly intense people, whose needs beat upon each other rather than finding satisfaction and fulfillment. The intensity of the marriage has been met in divorce by equal force, the factors of adultery notwithstanding. Mady becomes in effect the martyred adultress, and Herzog the humorous, tolerant, unwittingly pathetic cuckold. He wears his horns with bravado and rancor. Having been hoodwinked by his best friend, Valentine Gersbach, is only part of his woe. It is the manner in which Val and Mady have usurped the essence of his personal attributes which enrages him. Moreover, the second marriage has produced a precious daughter, June, and Herzog's strong sense of paternity is wounded, not only by the physical separation from his child, but by his impotence to cope with the situation over which Madeleine and Valentine have contrived almost absolute control. Robbed of the most vital aspects of parenthood, Herzog suffers even greater humiliation from the manner in which his personal attributes have been commandeered and recreated by his ex-wife and her concubine. For Mady has pursued the academic side of his intellect according to her own interests, (Slavic languages and literature), and Valentine, the once small-time radio announcer, has become the public intellectual in his own version of Herzog's personality.

After an attempted escape to Europe for solace and stability during which he gained neither, Herzog has returned to New York and is living irregularly in a run-down Westside apartment and giving a series of adult education lectures. One of his students becomes his current mistress and potential third wife. Ramona, a divorcee in her mid-thirties and proprietress of a Lexington Avenue florist shop, has an intensity more compatible with Herzog's than was Madeleine's. Of European-South American background, Ramona's is the intensity of loving and effective commitment that both gratifies and disconcerts Herzog who is not yet ready for a new commitment himself. The need to escape Ramona's affection for both their goods drives Herzog to another abortive attempt at respite with friends at Martha's Vineyard. Fleeing what seems to him a humiliating but genuinely offered dose of benevolence, Herzog returns to New York. Again he flees Ramona, but this time to settle accounts in his native Chicago where ex-wife and daughter, ex-friends Valentine and Phoebe Gersbach, other Herzog brothers and old friends live. Herzog's mission is ostensibly one of violence, but this too becomes an abortive disaster, and nearing the edge of a breakdown, he makes one last gesture of escape. This time it is to his run-down house on a large tract of property long unattended in Ludeyville, Massachusetts. Amid the neglected mementos of his past life with Madeleine, Herzog sifts through the dirt, disrepair, and disorder of his past in the solitude of the

Berkshires, writing out the last of his thought-messages to people living and dead, famous and only privately known. Here at least is a toe-hold on reality in the pastoral disorder, an improvement of some degree over the chaotic urban scene. The flood tides of anxiety begin to recede, and the messages cease. The ambiguous but sufficiently restored form of Herzog, the crisis-veteran, emerges as the novel ends.

DETAILED ANALYSIS AND COMMENTARY

STYLE AND TECHNIQUES: Unlike *The Adventures of Augie March*, *Herzog* is not an episodic novel, nor does it have the virtuosity of style that the earlier book had. The immediately detectable difference between the two prize-winning novels is the development of Mr. Bellow's style. In a form that critics still consider "anti-literary," *Herzog* shows a sophistication, refinement, and maturity of style that was wanting in the earlier work. Because *Herzog* is a full length exposition of a state of mind, its movement accrues not from the episodic adventures of the protagonist, but from a delicate manipulation of the details, past and present, of a man's life, which produce an integrated whole as much as a traditional plot or story line.

NOVEL OF EFFECT: However, the emphasis of *Herzog* is on effect, rather than storytelling. Hence, the novel concentrates on those elements which produce, implicitly and explicitly, a sense of immediacy and intensity. In *The Adventures of Augie March* the effect was motion—created by a running, brawling protagonist whose flamboyant narration of incident was of major importance as a story. The effect of *Herzog* is oppression—an abnormal state of mind—caused by circumstances of the past and present, related by a third-person with frequent intervals of first-person vocalizing by the protagonist. While there is as much license taken with language in the later novel, it is of a less defensive and more reflective tone. Augie was young and had to prove himself; Moses Herzog can afford to laugh at himself in his middle-age. There are sophistications of thought and speech patterns in *Herzog*, a more studied approach than the free-wheeling method of *Augie March*. The language of the more recent book is the richer for the character's experience as well as the author's. There are the enhancements of foreign phrases—particularly French and Yiddish. One might say in comparison that the style of *Herzog* is enriched by greater nuance and flavor of the language, as well as the development of the author in other works in the fifteen years between the two publications.

TECHNIQUES: Two outstanding techniques employed by Mr. Bellow in *Herzog* are the use of the flashback and the interior monologue. The term "flashback" can be understood by those familiar with that technique used in motion pictures—the brief exposure of an incident of the past in relation to the current scene. The interior monologue is a technique perfected by many authors such as James Joyce and Virginia Woolf by means of a device known as "stream of consciousness"; that is, the reader is allowed to observe the thought processes as they might occur in the character's subjective mind before they are distilled and refined by the objectivity of a third-person narrator. This technique provides an accurate frame of reference for the character's motivation and subsequent action. Used by Mr. Bellow in *Herzog*, these two techniques amply provide validity for the main character's condition and behavior. Since Herzog is isolated throughout most of the book, these techniques directly communicate the motivation and background of the character and make his behavior realistic rather than artificially manipulated by an obvious narrator/author. Interestingly enough, Mr. Bellow has amalgamated the techniques of the "stream of consciousness" novel and the "epistolary" (letter-writing to tell a story) novel in creating Herzog's interior monologue. By successful timing, the flashbacks and interior monologue provide the motion for the otherwise limited narrative. Again, as in *The Adventures of Augie March*, the author provides an even more vast intellectual framework for the exposition of the novel. Allusions of philosophy, literature, psychology, history, and the Bible are plentiful. These help support the character of Herzog as a "thinking man" whose intellect becomes his means of salvation.

THEMES—"ZEITGEIST": A word imported from German which frequently finds expression in modern literary discussion is the term "zeitgeist." What it means literally is "timetaste"; however, what it means idiomatically (as it is most often applied) is "temper of the times." Thematically, it might be said that *Herzog*, despite its major focus on character, is actually representative of the temper of the current era, and more specifically, the nineteen-sixties as illustrated in the personage of Moses Herzog. The overall statement of the novel is primarily concerned with the situation of the modern man of sensibility and intellect. This is shown in Herzog's wistful reflection on the values of the past and his ultimately regenerated hope for the future, both of which are distilled in a crisis of the present. The "piercing" questions that Herzog asks are those of the contemporary man oppressed by his world of seemingly suffocating details and circumstances which create a temporary impasse and must be overcome lest he fall prey to boredom and despair. The "zeitgeist" theme is illustrated in the imaginary letters written by Herzog, especially those to scholars, statesmen, and philosophers. As Herzog reflects on the lost values of the past, the loneliness and confused despair of the present, he concludes that the hope of the future lies in the power of the human intellect to achieve salvation and restoration of order. The crisis of Herzog as a representative of his times is an insufferable intensity of ideas which need reorganization in order to become viable factors against the anxiety of the age.

IDEALS VS. REALITY: The method by which Mr. Bellow generates the effect of the "zeitgeist" theme is that of creating subordinate motifs in the form of conflicts. Among those myriad conflicts which beset modern man is that of his ideals versus the brutal realities of life. Herzog is aware of both. He pursues his ideals in the form of scholarship and the attempted application of great ideas, only to find that his flesh is weak where his spirit would be strong. Moreover, he is aware of reality's effect only after the fact, despite the lectures of friends such as lawyers Simkin and Himmelstein who attempt to be his "reality teachers." Painfully aware that the ideals of the Enlightenment and nineteenth-century philosophers no longer maintain, he engages in combat with reality in search of a balance or a new order which he feels must be distilled through the agent of man.

INTELLECT VS. EMOTION: Another aspect of conflict is the war between the intellect and the emotions. The battleground for this is in the field of human relationships. By now, Herzog ought to be an expert, but here once again, the mind is strong where the passions are vulnerable. Intellectually, he is aware of his characteristically subordinate position in love relationships. But he cannot avoid man's need of woman, his own need of love, and the contemporary factors which make the psychology of love a precarious issue. Hence, his previous disasters serve only to drive him on to further explorations of love with the possible hope of achieving intellectual and emotional balance. His sophistication of experience does not exempt him from emotional jeopardy in each new relationship in which there is a new struggle for mutual identification. He must learn to love both wisely and well. His first marriage (to Daisy) illustrates the prevalence of intellect; his second marriage (to Madeleine) represents an imbalance favoring the emotions. Neither has been successful. The relationship with Ramona indicates a possibility for a relationship of balanced intellect and emotion.

VALUES: Because of his scholarly profession, Herzog has had an opportunity to explore the values of other periods of history. What he has come to realize is that old values no longer maintain. In fact, as far as he is concerned, the values of the past have been reversed. Morals, ethics, relationships, even personal roles have been reversed and the changeover has yet to be synthesized. Interestingly enough, it is in this respect that one of the more ironic twists is presented. As a professor of intellectual and cultural history, Herzog is also purported to be an expert on values—past, present, and future. But here his confusion is consummate, as revealed by his many unfinished scholarly projects. Moreover, it is in his work that we are given to understand his position intellectually as an anti-romantic. He has studied various aspects of romanticism (that yearning for perfection and idealistic reaction to the turmoil of the nineteenth century as exhibited in philosophy and the arts) and judged them as a basis for the contemporary neurosis. Herzog claims to be a champion of the Enlightenment (a term applied to an eighteenth-century philosophical movement generally characterized by rationalism). In all he does, Herzog is far more the romantic than the rationalist. Yet, his salvation will come through his intellect, despite the romantic elements of his personality; that is, intellect will prevail. However, it is not via

the philosophies of the Enlightenment that his intellect will find
a way. What he realizes is that the past is dead and the history
of the present will determine contemporary philosophy. He
must live in the present, intellectually and emotionally.

PUBLIC VS. PRIVATE: An important issue in the novel is the
conflict between man's public and private worlds. The encroachment of the public on the private life of man is illustrated at great length both by the circumstances and people
that affect Herzog and in the imaginary correspondence of the
protagonist in which a historical basis is given for this particular phenomenon of contemporary life. Herzog himself cannot
really escape the pressures of the external world, as evidenced
by the people in his life whose constant influence has driven
him into his current crisis; neither can contemporary man escape the burdens of society by self-willed exile. The private self
can barely be located, and even if this is achieved, the private
self often is a loathesome creature who needs the encum-
brances he has sought to escape. The accommodation of the private to the public self is another of the "piercing" questions
with which Herzog struggles.

THEMATIC SUMMARY: In achieving a representation of the
dilemma of contemporary man, Mr. Bellow has utilized the
motivation of conflict. Herzog, the protagonist, is buffeted intellectually and emotionally between a vast series of opposites
which illustrate the impotence of man to cope adequately with
the crisis of modern times. Everything seems to be a question
of polemics resulting in the schizoid tendency of our generation.
The issues are the "piercing" questions which become just one
"overwhelming question," as in T.S. Eliot's *The Love Song of
J. Alfred Prufrock*. Among the conflicts are the identifiable
ones such as 1) love vs. hatred, 2) intellect vs. emotion, 3)
chaos vs. order, 4) the private individual vs. the public self as
one of the masses, 5) the old, defined but now inapplicable
values vs. the new, undefined but existentially functional values,
6) cowardice vs. heroism, 7) ideals vs. reality. There are many
more subtle conflicts in the novel which, combined with the
more obvious ones, culminate in the "overwhelming" question
of being vs. non-being. As the issues reach their most fevered

pitch in the crisis of Herzog's life, a quiescence sets in which allows the state of being to prevail even if it is not totally clarified or resolved. It is the acquisition of this spiritual peace —transient as it may be—which is the goal of modern man. The means are not always clear, but the end is a worthwhile goal in itself and must be achieved if man is to survive.

SOURCES AND INFLUENCES: Commenting on *Herzog*, Mr. Bellow said that this novel represented a "break from victim literature which shows the impotence of ordinary man in whom anomaly, estrangement, and the collapse of humanism render all hope in virtuosity." The author characterized his previous works as "victim literature." If one adopts Mr. Bellow's remark as a tool for understanding *Herzog*, it becomes evident that this novel differs considerably from earlier ones in the characterization of the protagonist and the outcome of his crisis. While the protagonists of the previous novels have been set on the road to salvation and greater self-awareness by means of action, Moses Herzog is always self-aware, and is looking for spiritual salvation by means of the intellect as a prerequisite to action. Herzog's "angst" (or "soul-sickness") is far more a symptom of an intellectual disease directly related to the world in which he is over-involved than a sympton of alienation. Moreover, Herzog is too self-aware and too well-informed intellectually to be driven blindly toward an unconscious goal as are the earlier protagonists. Presented as Herzog's serious philosophical quest, the novel is endowed with elements of high comedy and tragedy by the dramatization of the quest controlled by intellect.

INTELLECTUAL REFERENTS: As so often in Mr. Bellow's fiction, *Herzog*, even more than previous works, contains vast quantities of intellectualism. Throughout the work there are references to various fields of formalized knowledge, such as literature, psychology, history, religion (the Old and New Testaments) and philosophy. In addition to formal intellectual disciplines, there is much Jewish folk wisdom as well as the sagacity and sophistication of the urbane observer of contemporary life. Mr. Bellow's sources are myriad. Borrowing from great men of ideas and emotions, the author has compiled and synthesized the notions of Nietzsche, Whitehead, Freud, Buber and Hobbes by employing the protagonist's occupation as a professor as a vehicle for this work which belongs to the genre of the novel of ideas.

HUMANISM: Traditionally, we think of *humanism* in modern parlance as referring to Renaissance Humanism, that is to say, the philosophy or attitude which grew out of the Renaissance in Europe as a reaction to Medieval fear and superstition. In general, this concept means an emphasis on man's capacity for free will as the factor of his own perfection. The social and political philosophers of the Enlightenment took the concepts of Renaissance Humanism even further as a weapon against feudalism. Historically, then, we might consider the various connotations of humanism as those elements by which man has strived for freedom from subservience in order to attain perfectibility in this world. For the doctrines of humanism, while not necessarily anti-religious, are concerned with worldly achievement rather than the medieval notion of striving only for perfection in the next world. What Mr. Bellow has attempted in *Herzog* is to sift through the phases of humanistic thought in an effort to come to terms with an operative humanism for the contemporary man. Moses Herzog is more than anything else a humanist, concerned with man in this world, desperate for the values, ideals, and methods by which the individual may find self-acceptance and regain the ground that humanism has lost in the disasters and upheavals of modern history. That Herzog groans and suffers is less a condition of self-pity than a lament for mankind. Unlike Augie or Henderson, Herzog doesn't want to be a superman, nor does he assert himself as "dos kleine menschele": both types represent that sort of "victim literature" of Mr. Bellow's previous works. For both types, the only answer is the grand exertion of personality over the ubiquitous perils of existence. Herzog is the humanist—the man who, in saving himself, would save mankind—sifting and sorting through the great ideas of the past. He is seeking, intellectually and emotionally, that formula by which man can reassert his lost values and realistically endow life once again with its worthwhileness and possible earthly perfectibility.

CHARACTER ANALYSES

MOSES HERZOG: A middle-aged scholar, itinerant professor, and intellectual, Moses Herzog suffers and groans, jokes and intellectualizes his way through a crisis in his life. Following the dramatic circumstances surrounding his second divorce, he attempts, in the metaphor of his own life, to piece together a workable set of values for the civilization that has produced the public and private disasters which he has survived. Seeking an intellectual and emotional balance, he comments on his own life and mentally researches the history of civilization in an attempt to regain a now lost or inoperative humanism. Herzog is a man of our time, an individual looking for both self-acceptance and the personal worth of man which has diminished. Imposed upon by circumstance and encroaching personal relationships, Herzog seeks seclusion as a respite from the oppressive chaos out of which he would like to re-establish order. In all the glory and foolishness of his intellectual and emotional intensity, Herzog communicates by means of imaginary and real but unsent letters to numerous people, great and unknown, past and present. These letters are significant, for they explore, challenge, and protest the values of the age in which the individual is no longer a positive factor. Herzog's field of scholarship is intellectual history, and he reveals his possession of distilled aspects of many great movements of thought, particularly those tenets of the eighteenth and nineteenth century which are the basis of modern history.

Prodigality: Considering his life from the roots of his Jewish heritage, he bemoans the loss of Old Testament strength of character and the subsequent weakening of his people's adherence to ancient values, particularly in the twentieth century. Recounting the Herzog family history, he looks for those elements which have formed his strengths and weaknesses. Haunted by an impotent sense of duty to both God and the Herzog family, he acknowledges his prodigality on the grounds of the modern human condition which he feels affects us more than God and family values.

Marriage: Recalling his marriages, he easily accounts for the failure of the first, but he cannot dismiss the failure of the second from which he is recovering. As the loser in the contest of egos between himself and his recent former wife, he begins to analyze and synthesize cause and effect in an attempt to formulate a much needed new approach to love. Full of anger and sadness, he cannot yet justify emotionally the way things have turned out, yet he accepts the situation and its meaning on the basis of reason and intellect. Denied the role of husband and father, he considers his appropriateness for either part. He feels even more out of place in the renaissance of bachelorhood. Herzog reflects on his relationships with his friends. Has he always been sincere in fulfilling the obligations of friendship? Have his friends fulfilled theirs to him?

Weighing the Balance: Although he has tried, his efforts seem to have fallen ironically short in his roles as scholar, friend, husband, son, parent, lover and Jew. But neither has he been a complete flop. It is only that he has tried either too much or too little. Hence, his present condition and the value crisis which will hopefully result in answers to his "piercing questions of life" and an indication of the next step. A figure less picaresque than Augie March, Herzog is the monumental but unheroic protagonist of intellect and sensibility for whom the answers to his "piercing questions" lie somewhere between earthy "potato love" and abstracted scholarship.

MADELEINE HERZOG: Presented primarily from Herzog's point of view, Madeleine Pontritter Herzog is a talented, attractive but highly neurotic woman whose intensity conflicts with that of her ex-husband. Competitive, financially irresponsible, given to fettishes (such as religion and super-organization), and adulterous, Mady seems to be the characteristic portrayal of the cruel and faithless woman in Herzog's still prejudiced view. However, in the more objective commentary of the other characters, she is no more than a sensitive, somewhat confused, forceful and fascinating woman. The basis for much of her neuroticism is her ultra-bohemian family background; she is the daughter of a bizarre theatrical director and his slavishly devoted wife. Despite her unusual attitudes, Mady is reputedly a good mother, adequate scholar, and social charmer. Her powers of hate and love are revealed in her relationships with Herzog (before, during, and after marriage) and with her lover Valentine Gersbach. Driven as is Herzog into a psychological crisis, her emotional pyrotechnics and peculiar behavior do not seem extremely abnormal in the given context. Her function in the novel is as a foil for the reader's ultimate judgment of Herzog himself. As the immediate cause of his suffering, she provides the realistic basis of the metaphor by which the author conducts Herzog's cosmic contemplations. That is, Mady provides the immediate conflict through which the other conflicts in the novel are presented. And lastly, she represents an inexorable reality to which Herzog must adjust.

VALENTINE GERSBACH: An even more representational figure than Madeleine, Valentine, the one-legged radio-announcer with flaming auburn hair, is never directly portrayed in the novel. He exists largely by virtue of his powerful image in the conversations of the others and the mind of Moses Herzog. As in other works by Mr. Bellow, Gersbach is the heroic-vitalist of the novel. He has overcompensated for his physical deficiency by what seems to be disproportionate abundance of spiritual power. He is the great doer of all things with an immense capacity for feeling, as evidenced by descriptions of his boisterous laughter, frequent tears, and magnified sympathies. Noted for his grandiloquence and theatrical personality, Gersbach is logically a character more of reputation than actuality in the novel. His attempts to untangle the Herzogs' marital difficulties have succeeded only in providing a vacancy that he is only too willing to fill. By involving himself in the needs of the Herzogs, he fulfills his own role—he becomes the product of the necessity he has created. Thus, in Herzog's absence from Chicago, Gersbach has become a version of his former best friend. But notice that the version is a corruption rather than an improvement, even though the role is magnified. In becoming Mady's lover, Valentine is the head of two households, but deficient in both; as an intellectual, he is an entrepreneur and an outsider, not a scholar nor a member of the intelligentsia. While he commands awe, he foregoes respect. He functions in the novel as an antithetical figure to Herzog.

RAMONA: A divorcee in her middle thirties, Ramona is presently Herzog's mistress and potential third wife. From Buenos Aires, she is a Jewess of mixed European lineage in whom culture, emotion, shrewdness and physical attributes are favorably combined. Ramona is experienced in love and capable of the devotion and independence that Herzog finds attractive and necessary although he flees her aggressiveness in fear of a serious relationship for which he is not quite ready. She seems to combine old world values with American modernity in a way that Herzog finds pleasing but is not ready to accept completely until he has clarified his own position with respect to his relationships with others. A sophisticated New Yorker, Ramona demonstrates a capacity for certain middle-class pleasantries that constitute order and stability. Having indulged in her share of unconventional romances, she is readier than Herzog for a relatively conventional cosmopolitan way of life. Ramona's persistence in her love for Herzog, although deeply appreciated, drives him away temporarily, but succeeds in holding him even at a distance. He admires her courage in taking matters into her own hands where he is concerned, despite whatever trepidation may lurk below the surface of her efficacy. Her confidence and dignity reflect the nascent rejuvenation of Herzog's own. She is portrayed as an influential factor in the reshaping of Herzog's new world although there is no acknowledged commitment within the scope of the novel. Her function in the book is to provide for the possibilities that exist for Herzog in the formulation of his steps beyond the crisis.

SIMKIN AND HIMMELSTEIN: Lawyers, Machiavellians, and "reality-instructors" of Herzog, Simkin in New York and Sandor Himmelstein in Chicago provide the protagonist with jet blasts of brute philosophy from the other side of the humanistic argument. Somewhat reminiscent of Einhorn and Mintouchian in *The Adventures of Augie March*, these men are the protectors and harsh instructors of Herzog in the ways of the beast known as man. Their profession as lawyers has provided them with opportunities to observe the savage behavior of people under extremes of pressure. While their philosophies are coarse and repugnant to Herzog, his cognizance of them provides a balance for his own inherent optimism. Simkin is more like the Mintouchian of the earlier work; Himmelstein, a cripple as was Einhorn, is likewise an overcompensating heroic vitalist. Both lawyers are ironically so involved in society that they may live beyond it, whereas in contrast, Herzog is so abstracted from it that he has become unwittingly over-involved.

CRITICAL REACTION TO *HERZOG*

PUBLISHING HISTORY: When *Herzog* appeared as a published novel (after 15 revisions) in the autumn of 1964 (sections had been published earlier in magazines), critics hailed it as a major literary event of the times. It was subsequently awarded the International Literary Prize and the National Book Award for Fiction (Mr. Bellow's second, the first was for *The Adventures of Augie March*). Aside from critical acclaim, *Herzog* was overwhelmingly accepted by the public, occupying a place on "best seller" lists for many months. Within a year, the novel had had seventeen printings in hard-cover form; it was released in paperback late in 1965.

CRITICAL CONSENSUS: Among the major contemporary critics and men of letters praising *Herzog* were Granville Hicks, Irving Howe, Philip Rahv, and Julian Moynahan. Major periodicals without identified reviewers, such as *Time* and *Newsweek* magazines, favored the novel, as did the individual reviewers of more specialized magazines of limited circulation. While the consensus of the reviewers was favorable, the main objection to the novel was the oppressiveness of the protagonist's suffering. Some critics felt that this was a major flaw in the work. Herzog's suffering became a kind of inverted joke among some intellectuals. However, the brilliance of technique and style were considered the signal achievements of the work. The public reacted enthusiastically, whether favorably or unfavorably on individual bases, as indicated by the mass volume of sales and the quantity of correspondence which Mr. Bellow received from readers.

INDIVIDUAL CRITICS: Professor Irving Howe, writing his review of *Herzog* for the *New Republic*, called the work "an extremely, if unevenly brilliant novel" and the author "a virtuoso of fictional technique and language." What Mr. Howe considered to be Mr. Bellow's major achievements with this novel were the mastery of the art of timing in a blend of past and present which produced a controlled rush of narrated experience and endowed the work with effects of immediacy and intensity. The flaws as Mr. Howe saw them lay in the over-focusing of Herzog's character which he claimed caused the protagonist to become too enclosed in his withdrawal and thus too confused. Critic Granville Hicks wrote in the *Saturday Review* that *Herzog* resembled Thomas Mann's *Dr. Faustus* in the challenge of its presenting the dramatization of a philosophical quest. Mr. Hicks, along with critic Philip Rahv (editor of the *Partisan Review*) concurred in their evaluations of *Herzog* and in their belief that its publication made Saul Bellow the leading writer of fiction in America at the present time.

OTHER WORKS BY SAUL BELLOW

SEIZE THE DAY

Tommy Wilhelm, the protagonist of Mr. Bellow's fourth novel, (published three years after *The Adventures of Augie March*), is the portrait of a first-rate slob who hates his nature but is unable to change it. The moving story of the funny-sad Tommy takes place in the area of upper-Broadway at a residential hotel in New York City. Having left his wife and his job, Tommy is alienated—a condition by now a familiar feature of the author's works. Down to his last few hundred dollars, Tommy begins to experience the facts of life that he has avoided for most of his forty-odd years. He must figure out where to go and what to do while he still has the opportunity for a choice. Confounding possible decisions are a wife who will not give him a divorce, two sons whom he loves, and a father who will not give him a shred of sympathy. Watching the disintegration of his self-image creates even further anxiety. The end of everything must be resolved in the beginning of something—but what?

A BORN LOSER: Unlike Bellow's other major characters, Tommy Wilhelm is presented as one who has a greater potential for failure than for success. His limitations are too severe for heroic vitalism, fatalistic determination overcome by personality, or intellectual salvation. In short, Tommy is a born loser, more an overgrown boy than a man. What enables the reader to become sympathetically involved with him at all is his cognizance of his inadequacies and his forthrightness (bordering on virtuosity) about trying. Having reached the lowest point of his internal and external resources, he remains heroic by virtue of his refusal to accept defeat.

SEEKS DISASTER: Tommy's frustration constitutes the most important action of the novel. He has a penchant for courting and winning disaster. Like many down-and-outers, he lives always on the brink of "getting a break," only to find himself broken. Fully conscious of his own responsibility for failing in life, he lives in the imaginary world of possible success. His current scheme for getting lucky revolves around the investment of his last few hundred dollars. One of the other residents at the hotel, a Dr. Tamkin, advises him what stocks are worth speculation. Tommy and Dr. Tamkin go to the local stock exchange every morning and watch the figures as they are flashed from Wall Street. Day after day they watch, waiting for the "right moment"—the point at which they will pull their money out at a great profit. Day after day, the tension builds and Tommy comes nearer to the brink of disaster.

FEAR OF CYNICISM: The conditions of Tommy's investment are indicative of his character and the events of the past which have led to his present state. Tommy is one who trusts. While he is not naive, he is neither ambitious nor thorough enough to investigate the risks he takes. Most of his risks are made through people of questionable character. Tommy would sooner trust to their good intentions, convinced by the power of their rhetoric, than to request references or employ other means of investigation. He prefers to go on believing that these people will bring him fame and fortune in spite of the fact that their reputations are somewhat shady. In this way he can fight what he fears most—the cynicism of the world. His current investment with Tamkin is reminiscent of the investment of his career some twenty years earlier with a movie talent scout named Maurice Venice. Easily impressed by this braggart's sales pitch, Tommy threw away his college education for the chance to be a star. Like his investment with Tamkin, the earlier decision came about after endless debates with himself. But Tommy has always chosen the thing his intuition said was wrong. Most of these decisions have been based on his desire to be something other than what his own nature has made him. As his father puts it: "You fool, you clunk, you Wilky!"

FATHER VS. SON: Among Tommy's other problems is one more basic—and possibly causal—his father. Also a resident at the same hotel, Dr. Adler, Tommy's father, is a constant reminder of all that the son is not and never will be. Successful in practice and now retired, Dr. Adler is a venerable figure among the residents of the hotel. He is of the old, European school which "taught" that one works hard, looks and acts right, and stays on a straight path. He does not believe in taking undue risks nor in contemplating freakish lucky breaks. Now in his old age, he is resting on the laurels of his hard work and straight living. He is wealthy, still handsome, and orderly in everything he does. He would prefer not to be made aware of his son's problems, for he plans to live out his remaining years in peace. He will tolerate his son's company only to a certain point. When Tommy wants his father's sympathy, Dr. Adler becomes inflexible. He will not become responsible for his son, neither lending money nor emotion. He wants "nobody on his back" and advises Tommy to share that philosophy. He sees the answers to his son's problems as clear-cut and simple: take action! Tommy's characteristic inability to take any action, or else the wrong action, is a source of great conflict between the father and son. Dr. Adler feels that Tommy makes a career out of his troubles, and Tommy accuses his father of making a career out of waiting for death. This conflict instills in Tommy the notion that it is his business in life to carry the burden of shame and impotence, that his purpose in life is to make mistakes and to suffer for them.

RESOLUTION: Taken in once more by a shyster, Tommy is now without funds. The world has beaten him and his only recourse is death. But Tommy realizes that he loves this crazy, chaotic world too much, that the people in it are his brothers and sisters, and that he does have a life to live, albeit a disfigured and now ruined one. Now that all the practical experiences have been tried and have failed there is one thing left —the mystical experience. The hero who can run and brawl no longer wanders through the city on a metaphysical mission. In the least likely manner, he finds the answer to the quest for his heart's ultimate need. The passion swelling within him is an affirmation of the need, not to die, but to live. He now sees his previous attempts at non-existence—his attempts to live the lives of various characters he would be, rather than the one life of the person he is—as a means of self-annihilation. Living as himself is the only true way to express his confirmed love of life. Thus, his final act reveals his ability to accept himself. It is in that moment of mystical illumination that Tommy can follow the advice of Tamkin and "seize the day."

HENDERSON THE RAIN KING

A COMPLEX NOVEL: Mr. Bellow's fifth novel, which preceded *Herzog* by five years, is a complex work in which many of the author's previous themes are brought together and given expression of a new and different sort. *Henderson the Rain King*, as a predecessor to *Herzog*, resembles the later work in its philosophical complexity and maturity of attitude. It is a far more intellectualized work than the earlier four novels, yet it is consistent in the virtuosity of style for which Mr. Bellow has become known. The familiar thesis of man's desire to live—but how?—is the main theme of the work.

EARLY THESIS STATEMENT: Henderson, the hero, does not need to wait until the novel's end to learn that above all else man wants to live. Nor does Henderson have to wait very long to find out what his problem is nor how to go about solving it. The novel is sustained not by the vehicle of the extravagant adventures of Connecticut millionaire Eugene Henderson in Africa; but by the process of self-transcendence which he undergoes in order to sustain his already avowed affirmation of life and which is represented by his adventures. The conflict is stated in the words of that little voice inside Henderson which keeps saying, "I want, I want." The progress of the novel is the progress of Henderson's transformation from a state of "becoming" to one of "being." Augie March was left, at the end of that novel, in a state of becoming. In *Herzog* the protagonist has already achieved the state of being but must learn how to continue in that condition after surviving a number of disasters. In relation to these two novels, *Henderson the Rain King* reveals a character between the two conditions—becoming and being.

AN UNUSUAL CHARACTER: Eugene Henderson, unlike any of the other protagonists of Mr. Bellow's fiction, is decidedly non-Jewish and non-urban; he is a Yankee millionaire from Connecticut with "all the advantages." However, like other Bellovian heroes, he is an outcast of sorts. He is, moreover, presented as more of an heroic vitalist than other protagonists of the author's fiction. A physical and spiritual giant, he is a titan of energy and other resources. He has power over all he surveys in the material and physical sense. Self-educated beyond his Ivy League diploma, he has amassed vast quantities of knowledge. He has undertaken all sorts of activities for the sake of diversion, such as pig-farming, hunting, playing the violin, drinking, and suffering. Henderson, unlike Herzog, does not suffer oppressively; rather, he suffers tremendously—the way he does everything else. His immense size is the metaphor for the immensity of his chaos. At the age of fifty-five, he has been married twice, sired five children, travelled extensively, amassed even more money than his birthright provided, and lived life with a phenomenal vigor and intensity. His life is comprised of a series of hilarious and bizarre, yet poignant, escapades.

TO AFRICA: Having searched through books for the philosophical answer to satisfy the "I want, I want" voice within him, he has been unsuccessful. His wildly intense hobbies at home have not provided him with the fulfillment he craves. He has a reputation in his community for being a rather fearsome, unkillable giant. His myth among the local gentry is not exactly a favorable one. This distresses his wife Lily, who would prefer to establish a conventional position for herself and her family. Her main fear, however, is that Gene will shoot himself in the head as he often threatens to do in moments of acute dissatisfaction. Then the "day of tears and madness" arrives, and Henderson feels obliged to leave. As a kind of pilgrimage of penance, he decides to go to Africa.

AMONG THE ARNEWI: Henderson's first sojourn is with a pacifist tribe known as the Arnewi. It is during his stay with these people that he hears the phrase "Grun-to-molani," or man-want-to-live; he becomes possessed by this principle. He attempts as an expression of good will, to rid the tribe's water supply of a plague of frogs, and accidentally blows it up. His ideal of service has failed here, and he feels obliged to leave, although his hosts do not express any hostility toward him. Leaving the Arnewi with the phrase "Grun-to-molani" and the concept of "Bittahness" (the ultimate condition of happiness), Henderson journeys on with his faithful guide Romilayu. His sense of failure has made him abject. He has not yet found the best way to live.

THE WARIRI: Wandering through the African jungle, Henderson and Romilayu come upon the tribe of the Wariri whose young King Dahfu takes Henderson as his protege. In a sense, the migration from the Arnewi to the Wariri is like the casting out from Eden of Adam and Eve. The Wariri are a warring tribe, fraught with political intrigue. Nevertheless, Henderson becomes an important figure in the tribe—their Rain King—for having accomplished a feat of superior strength. As the Rain King he must remain with the Wariri and perform his ceremonial functions of dispensing water. However, there is more to his life as the young king's protege.

KING DAHFU: The King is serving his probationary period in that office. He has certain duties to perform before his title is unchallenged. An intellectual, mystic, and philosopher, young Dahfu decides to show Henderson the secrets of his self-fashioned religion. Dahfu is an amalgam of three important intellectual concepts represented historically by King David, Friedrich Nietzsche, and Wilhelm Reich. Respectively, they represent the giver of laws, the concept of the superman, and the principles of somatic psychology. Dahfu attempts, through a series of spiritual exercises, to teach Henderson to contain humiliations, overcome fear, and to empty himself in order to become a man again. This last aspect is an adaptation of Nietzsche's treatise, *Thus Spake Zarathustra*. It is difficult for Henderson to learn these concepts. However, he senses that if he is successful, he will have quieted the "I want, I want" voice and will then have achieved a state of Being.

THE INHUMAN FIRE: Like Henderson, Dahfu is a fugitive from civilization who has returned from his university years in the city to find the reality principle among his fellow tribesmen. The Wariri are lion-worshipers, and through various rites, Dahfu attempts to teach Henderson how to assume and absorb the qualities of his pet lioness. He tells Henderson, "She will make consciousness shine. She will burnish you." That is to say, the lioness is Being, the end of Becoming. Henderson is successful in a limited fashion. He overcomes his fear of the lioness to some extent. In meeting the non-human, he discovers that the inhuman fire is at the center of his own humanity.

DEATH: One of the young king's tasks is to find the lion that contains the spirit of his father, the former king. Here the Reality principle is put to the test. This is not a pet lioness but a wild, savage male lion. Dahfu has accused Henderson of being a great avoider. In combat with the lion, Henderson can no longer avoid the Real, which in this case is Death. The lion kills Dahfu, but Henderson kills the lion. He learns that "Grun-to-molani" means going on living despite the death-dealing Real.

HARMONY: Having asserted his Being over the Real, Henderson now feels that he has achieved the harmony he has travelled to Africa to acquire. For Henderson, harmony is the Neitzschean notion of self-transcendence based on freedom. Henderson has learned what it is to contain freedom. He has accomplished the transformation of suicidal violence into love. His new freedom enables him to resurrect his old wish to attend medical school. Now that that dream is possible, Henderson's affirmation occurs en route home from Africa while the plane is refueling at Newfoundland: "I guess it was my turn now to move, so I went running—leaping, leaping, pounding, and tingling over the pure white lining of the gray Arctic silence."

ESSAY QUESTIONS AND ANSWERS

1. What is the function of the "personalist hero" in Mr. Bellow's novels?

ANSWER: Most of Mr. Bellow's protagonists are oppressed by the weight and clutter of existence, therefore, it becomes essential that radical self-assertion take place in order to overcome the chaos. That is, in order for the character to escape the burdens of fates and schemes other than his own, he must exercise his personality over and above all things. The function of this "personalist" hero is to exhibit courage in the face of the perils of existence. This courage becomes the foundation of his freedom. Often, the exercise of personality becomes an ironic element in the novel. In a way, the personalist becomes a mockery of himself, an example of the absurdity of the self in a world that denies individuality. It is then that bravado becomes the mask of bravery. However, the true function of the personalist hero is to secure the right to exist. The self-assertion becomes an axis on which is to be balanced the involvement of love and an independent fate. It is through the personality that the opposing forces will be reconciled.

2. What is meant by "victim" literature in respect to Mr. Bellow's novels?

ANSWER: Such characters as Tommy Wilhelm (*Seize the Day*), Joseph (*Dangling Man*), and Asa Leventhal (*The Victim*) are representative of heroes who have been overcome or victimized by circumstance. They are ordinary men who represent the impotence of the individual to avoid estrangement from life. They are men whose inability or lack of desire to take action has allowed circumstance to crowd in upon them and force them to sacrifice themselves to humanity in order to survive. They are men whose sense of self has been crippled by avoiding the responsibility of specific action; they would sooner remain passive and rail at the world for the chaos it produces which suffocates and annihilates. When the chaos has all but driven these "victims" mad, they must take action. They must accept responsibility for themselves in terms of love and self-sacrifice. Thus it is that Tommy affirms life by weeping, Joseph by sacrificing his freedom, and Asa by taking action within the involvement he has ignored.

3. Might Mr. Bellow's protagonists be called "angry men"?

ANSWER: Unlike the "angry young man" literature of England and the United States which was prevalent in the 1950's, Mr. Bellow's novels show less anger and more philosophy. While the Bellow protagonists are engaged in a struggle for identity against overwhelming circumstances from within and without, they are less angry than the heroes of the other school of fiction. For one thing, Mr. Bellow's heroes are not especially concerned with social position nor with the acquisition of money. They mainly want to know what is the best to live. Although they may be dour (like Joseph or Asa Leventhal), they are more concerned with finding a way out of their self-imprisonment or crisis than in taking out their frustrations on society. Their goal is one of self-transcendence, not social mobility. They begin in a somewhat disillusioned fashion and end in a condition of enlightenment, whereas the "angry young men" are usually idealists who become disillusioned and bitter at the mockery of life. However, both types of novels may be considered novels of protest—Mr. Bellow's fiction protesting and finding a solution to the condition of man, the "angry young man" school protesting and rendering a scathing judgment on mankind.

4. One of the criticisms that has been levelled at Mr. Bellow's novels is that while they exhibit great virtuosity of technique, they often lack discipline. Which novels seem to merit this criticism and which do not? Explain why.

ANSWER: "Virtuosity" is defined as great technical skill; it may be said that Mr. Bellow's virtuosity is apparent in the presentation of his characters. His novels are lacking in discipline, however, in those areas in which theme becomes subordinate to character and a gimmick must be used to bring the two into focus. For instance, *Dangling Man*, for all its complex presentation of character and problem, is enclosed short of action. *The Adventures of Augie March* has almost too much action to end. Moreover, the theme is extended beyond the necessity of the action. Therefore, the novel seems to go on repetitively without resolution. It ends somewhat abruptly, as if its narrator has become tired of his own running and brawling adventures and waxed suddenly wise. *Henderson the Rain King* is full of tricks. It is as inflated as its hero. The adaptation of the philosophical principles which Mr. Bellow wishes to illustrate becomes a superimposition on the wild extravagances of Gene Henderson's life. That is, he must go to the ends of the earth to learn a philosophy lesson just because of the extravagance of his character. *Herzog*, technically the best novel so far, has its flaws of over-focused characterization and an oppressive theme of suffering. The most well-made novels of Mr. Bellow might be considered to be *The Victim* and *Seize the Day*. However, in dealing with the complex issues which he has selected for his novels, Mr. Bellow's sacrifice of discipline to substance is a flaw of minor significance.

BIBLIOGRAPHY
AND GUIDE TO FURTHER RESEARCH

WORKS BY SAUL BELLOW

NOVELS: *Dangling Man* (1944)
The Victim (1947)
The Adventures of Augie March (1953)
Seize the Day (1956)
Henderson the Rain King (1959)
Herzog (1964)

PLAYS: *The Upper Depths* (1963), produced on Broadway
The Last Analysis (1964) produced on Broadway
A Wen (1965), published in *Esquire* Magazine

OTHER WORKS: Short stories—(1940 to the present) appearing in small magazines.

The Noble Savage—(co-editor) a literary magazine, now discontinued.

Essays: "Recent American Fiction," (1963), a lecture (now in print) given for the Gertrude Clarke Whithall Poetry and Literature Fund. (U.S. Government Printing Office, Washington, D.C.)

Other comments in literature appear occasionally in current periodicals, such as the *New York Times Book Review, The New York Times Magazine,* and other magazines.

SHORT CRITICAL PIECES ON
SAUL BELLOW

Brustein, Robert, Review of *The Last Analysis* in *The New Republic*, October 24, 1964.

Capon, Robert F., Review of *Herzog*, in *America: The National Catholic Weekly Review*, March, 1965.

Clurman, Howard, Review of *The Last Analysis* in *The Nation*, October 22, 1964.

Hicks, Granville, Review of *Herzog* in the *Saturday Review*, September 19, 1964.

Howe, Irving, Review of *Herzog* in the *New Republic*, September 24, 1964.

Klein, Marcus, "A Discipline of Nobility: Saul Bellow's Fiction," *The Kenyon Review*, Spring, 1962.

————, *Life Magazine*, article on Saul Bellow and his work, October 30, 1964.

LITERARY HISTORY AND CRITICISM

Aldridge, John W., *After the Lost Generation* (New York: McGraw Hill Book Company, 1951). An examination of those writers who came after World War I.

————, *In Search of Heresy* (New York: McGraw Hill Book Company, 1956). An unusual approach to the fiction that followed World War II. Depth studies of Bellow, Salinger, and Styron.

Alter, Robert, *Rogue's Progress*: *Studies in the Picaresque Novel.* (Cambridge: Harvard University Press, 1964).

Booth, Wayne C., *The Rhetoric of Fiction* (Chicago: University of Chicago Press, 1963). A discussion of fictional techniques used by authors from the eighteenth century to the present.

Fiedler, Leslie, *Love and Death in the American Novel* (New York: Criterion Books, 1960). An examination of national characteristics on a critical and historical basis. An unusual approach to the subject.

Heiney, Donald, *Recent American Literature* (Great Neck, New York: Baron's Educational Series, 1955). A limited handbook of author's biographies, types of literature, synopses of works, and bibliographies.

Lewis, Richard W. B., *The Picaresque Saint*: *Representative Figures in Contemporary Fiction* (Philadelphia: J. B. Lippincott, 1959).

Thorp, Willard, *American Writing in the Twentieth Century* (Cambridge: Harvard University Press, 1960). Good for background study up to and including World War II. Emphasizes major developments in American writing from 1920-1950. Includes drama, poetry, and fiction.

Trilling, Lionel, *The Liberal Imagination* (New York: Viking Press, 1950). Essays on literature and society.

SUGGESTED TOPICS FOR
FURTHER STUDY

1. Social criticism in Bellow's novels.

2. The "Virtuoso" of fictional style and technique.

3. Comparison to other "quest" novels (such as works by William Styron, J.D. Salinger, James Joyce, and others).

4. The relationship between Saul Bellow and the philosophers of the Enlightenment.

5. Saul Bellow as a contemporary humanist.

6. Realism and Romanticism in the works of Saul Bellow.

7. Saul Bellow on the dilemma of contemporary man.

8. "Victim" literature of France and its effect on the novels of Saul Bellow.

9. The progress and development of a philosophy of life throughout the novels of Saul Bellow.

10. Saul Bellow as a "Jewish" writer compared to others (such as Bernard Malamud, Sholem Aleichem, Philip Roth, Isaac Bashevis Singer, etc.).

NOTES

NOTES

NOTES

NOTES

NOTES

NOTES

NOTES

MONARCH
NOTES AND STUDY GUIDES

ARE AVAILABLE AT RETAIL STORES EVERYWHERE

In the event your local bookseller
cannot provide you with other
Monarch titles you want—

ORDER ON THE FORM BELOW:

Simply send retail price, local
sales tax, if any, plus 25¢ to
cover mailing & handling.

Complete order form appears
on inside front & back covers for
your convenience.

IBM #	AUTHOR & TITLE	(exactly as shown on title listing)	PRICE
	PLUS ADD'L FOR POSTAGE		25¢
	GRAND TOTAL		

MONARCH® PRESS, a division of Simon & Schuster, Inc.
Mail Service Department, 1 West 39th Street, New York, N.Y. 10018

I enclose................................dollars to cover retail price, local sales tax,
plus mailing and handling.

Name_____

Address_____
(Please print)
4410

City_____State_____ Zip_____
Please send check or money order. We cannot be responsible for cash.